Better Homes and Gardens®

YOUR BATHS

© Copyright 1983 by Meredith Corporation, Des Moines, Iowa.
All Rights Reserved. Printed in the United States of America.
First Edition. Second Printing, 1986.
Library of Congress Catalog Number: 81-70038
ISBN: 0-696-02165-X

BETTER HOMES AND GARDENS® BOOKS

Editor: Gerald M. Knox
Art Director: Ernest Shelton
Managing Editor: David A. Kirchner

Associate Art Directors: Linda Ford Vermie,
Neoma Alt West, Randall Yontz
Copy and Production Editors: Marsha Jahns,
Nancy Nowiszewski, Mary Helen Schiltz, David A. Walsh
Assistant Art Directors: Harijs Priekulis, Tom Wegner
Senior Graphic Designers: Alisann Dixon, Lynda Haupert,
Lyne Neymeyer
Graphic Designers: Mike Burns, Trish Church-Podlasek,
Mike Eagleton, Deb Miner, Stan Sams, D. Greg Thompson,
Darla Whipple, Paul Zimmerman

Editor in Chief: Neil Kuehnl
Group Editorial Services Director: Duane L. Gregg

General Manager: Fred Stines
Director of Publishing: Robert B. Nelson
Director of Retail Marketing: Jamie Martin
Director of Direct Marketing: Arthur Heydendael

All About Your House: Your Baths

Project Editor: James A. Hufnagel
Associate Editor: Willa Rosenblatt Speiser
Assistant Editor: Leonore A. Levy
Contributing Senior Writer: Paul Kitzke
Copy and Production Editor: Mary Helen Schiltz
Building and Remodeling Editor: Joan McCloskey
Furnishings and Design Editor: Shirley Van Zante
Garden Editor: Douglas A. Jimerson
Money Management and Features Editor: Margaret Daly

Art Director: Linda Ford Vermie
Graphic Designers: Trish Church-Podlasek, Stan Sams

Contributing Editor: Jill Mead
Contributors: James Downing, Cathy Howard, Jean LemMon,
Jill Mead, Stephen Mead, Marcia Spires

Special thanks to William N. Hopkins, Bill Hopkins, Jr.,
Babs Klein, and Don Wipperman for their valuable contributions
to this book.

INTRODUCTION

As the smallest rooms in most houses, bathrooms pose some of the biggest decorating and re-modeling challenges. Tight quarters mean that just about every inch must look and work its best. When it comes to making changes, tile and fixtures seem to have the permanence of stone. And a bath's most essential element—water—courses unseen through pipes hidden somewhere behind the walls.

Your Baths covers it all, from fixing a dripping faucet to adding a luxurious new at-home spa. This book begins by showing you how to take an analytical look at your home's bath or baths. Then you'll see how a new paint job, wall covering, tile, window treatment, and other cosmetic changes can revitalize a tired but still service-able facility.

Or maybe the biggest problem with the baths at your house is that there simply aren't enough of them. Later chapters take you through the process of how to fit in or add on a new one, help you choose the right fixtures, and show exactly what's involved in a to-the-studs remodeling.

With almost 150 color photographs, plus dozens of drawings, floor plans, and charts, *Your Baths* explores just about every facet of a modern-day bathroom and tells how to upgrade its appearance, convenience, cleanability, and safety. There's even advice about outfitting a bath for a disabled person and, at the back of the book, a series of templates showing typical fixture layouts.

Your Baths is just one volume in the **ALL ABOUT YOUR HOUSE** series, a library of ideas, information, and inspiration compiled by the editors of Better Homes and Gardens. Each book in the series delves into a different area or aspect of your home and tells how you can make it truly special.

YOUR BATHS

CONTENTS

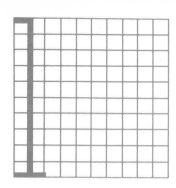

EVALUATING THE BATHROOMS AT YOUR HOUSE

At the 7 a.m. rush hour, your bathroom is probably the busiest place in the house. Perhaps *too* busy. If the one you have now can't handle the crowd—or simply doesn't work as efficiently as it should—then it's time to start thinking about improvements. As you start to review the possibilities, you're going to be surprised at the number of ways you can make your bath better than it is. Even in the tiniest house, your choices are many and varied. Read this first chapter to identify possible problems and solutions. When you come across an idea that sparks your imagination, turn to the chapter mentioned for more information.

HOW MANY PEOPLE USE YOUR BATH?

When you're sizing up the bathroom space you need, count noses. If the main—and maybe only—bath must accommodate Mom, Dad, and a handful of little ones, you should know some good space-planning tricks to serve them all.

Next, figure out how your bathroom works. Is it primarily a shower/bath/toilet area, or is it a place to shave or apply makeup? You may discover that too many things are going on at one time. In any case, your analysis will help determine if an entirely new bath is in order or whether a little expansion will do the job.

If you need more room, don't assume the only solution is to build a new bath or move. There are alternatives—space-stretching ideas—that allow several people to use a single bath at the same time. For example, with the addition of separate basins and mirrors, early-morning traffic jams may become nonexistent.

Chapter 4—"Getting a New Bath on Paper"—outlines basic advice for planning an extra bath or remodeling your present one. Chapter 6—"How to Add or Remodel a Bath"—then takes you, one step at a time, through the work needed to complete the job.

You may find, of course, that there just isn't room in the house—or in your budget—for a totally new bath. Chapter 8—"Bathroom Projects You Can Build"—suggests space-enhancing ideas to make better use of what you have.

If, on the other hand, your bath meets your present needs, and then some, maybe you have too much space. Take that extra room and transform it into a spa, exercise center, or garden bath. Chapter 7—"Treat Yourself to a Super Bath"—tells you how.

CAN YOU COMPARTMENTALIZE?

If you were to divide your bath into two separate areas—one for bathing and using the toilet, the other for washing up and grooming—would it work as well as having two baths? Generally, the answer is yes. By compartmentalizing different areas, you can produce a bath and a half in space that would otherwise be just a large single bath. When expansion is out of the question, this simple change may give you the results you're after.

If one person soaking in a tubful of warm water keeps the rest of the family out of the bathroom, it's time to think about how efficiently you're using the space. Why *can't* other family members use the bath at the same time? Is privacy the problem? If so, compartmentalizing the bath is a good solution. A bath as small as 5x8 feet can be divided into sections by adding a wall—with a door if you like—to separate the tub and toilet from the lavatory.

Side-by-side lavatories, an expansive mirror, and yards of counter space can produce a lavish makeup/shaving center like the one shown *opposite*. Both basins are well lighted and have storage below so two people can use them simultaneously. The dressing room/master bath area in the photo *at right* is a real workhorse: The space around the lavatory does double duty as a makeup/shaving center, while also providing light and ample mirrors for dressing. In both baths, a pocket door closes off the toilet, tub, and shower. One big advantage to arrangements like these is that moisture—principally steam from a tub or shower—can't migrate from the compartment to the rest of the bath.

You also can solve other problems by compartmentalizing. If, for example, two kids share a bath and are constantly locking each other out, divide it so both can use the facilities at once without interference. Chapter 4—"Getting a New Bath on Paper"—presents simple remodeling ideas you can use, and pages 72 and 73 show specific ways to make an existing bath more efficient.

DO THE KIDS HAVE A BATH OF THEIR OWN?

Splash! Most kids love to play in the water—from making waves in the wash basin to swirling around in the bathtub. Trouble is, they often turn the room upside down in the process. One solution is to make sure your bath is up to the challenge of handling small children. Another is to add an entirely new bath, a place where your kids can test the water to their heart's content.

When you're outfitting a bath for children, remember kids are people, too—only smaller. Everything you want them to use—soap, towels, water—should be an easy reach away. Vanities, in particular, must come down to their level. If it's not practical to refit the counters, build a semi-permanent "elevator" to raise your children up.

You may, however, find that a separate bath for the kids is a better idea. But where? Start your search right in their rooms. If a closet isn't essential, you might be able to squeeze a bath into it and add freestanding clothes storage to make up the difference. Similarly, an old mudroom may make a splendid new bath. For an older child, adding a new lavatory in his or her room might be enough to clear up

traffic in the main bath. Or if you already have an existing half bath, do as the owners did in the one shown *above:* Make it into a place for children only.

In any event, the best spot for a kids' bath is near where they spend their time—the bedrooms or the playroom. Chapter 4—"Getting a New Bath on Paper"—demonstrates several ways to find space in a variety of layouts.

Whatever your plans, choose materials for family and children's baths with care. Chapter 3—"Bathroom Surfaces Make a Material Difference"—pinpoints the most durable and easy to clean.

In addition, think about safety. On page 152 is a checklist that will help make your new bath a safe place to be, along with suggestions on how to childproof an existing bath.

HOW CAN YOU MAKE A GUEST BATH MORE INVITING?

Take a look at your guest bath. A *good* look. If it's not a pleasant sight, then maybe you should make some changes. True, it's tempting to ignore a room that's not used very often, but consider this: Putting together a well-groomed guest bath is not only a convenience for friends and relatives, it's also an important way to make them feel at home. Even if you don't have a bath just for guests, you can adapt other baths in your house to serve the same purpose.

A little ingenuity can provide the pep your room needs. Because the space is generally small, a guest bath offers an opportunity for some offbeat decorating. A fanciful lavatory, bright color scheme, or an antique display area all receive maximum exposure in this tiny spot. Chapter 2—"Give Your Bath a Fresh Look"—is packed with decorating ideas you can easily adapt to a smaller bath. And Chapter 3—"Bathroom Surfaces Make a Material Difference"—evaluates the best ways and means to bring those ideas to life.

If you don't have a separate bath for overnight guests, try using your secondary bath. Ideally, a guest bath is close to the room where overnighters sleep, but you can make an exception if another bath— one near the family room, for example—works better.

Keep a closet free for guests, and fill it with soft towels, sweet-smelling soaps, and other niceties. (See Chapter 9—"Stocking Your Bath"—for additional tips on what to include.) Assign towel hooks or bars to the guests; hands off to your kids.

Good lighting is also important. Shaving and applying makeup are delicate tasks your guests should never be in the dark when doing. Pages 40 and 41 describe the most effective ways to light up a bath.

If sharing won't do, and you really need another bath, consider adding a new one. Chapter 4—"Getting a New Bath on Paper"—contains helpful advice on how to plan the kind of bath you need.

WHAT MORE CAN YOU DO WITH A MASTER BATH?

Few family baths are large enough to be anything but what they are. A master bath, however, is something else. Here you have the room to create a glorious, adults-only oasis— a part of the master suite designed to serve as a soothing retreat from everyday life.

Start dreaming. Would you prefer to use a master bath for reading in a warm, bubble-filled tub? Or is a relaxing corner the perfect counterpoint to a relaxing shower? Whatever your desire, you can make room for it.

When planning, locate the necessities first—shower, tub, lavatory, and toilet. Then define and separate special areas. By compartmentalizing, you can, for example, build your oasis in a leftover corner.

If you have an especially large room, adapt part of it to your particular interests. Chapter 7—"Treat Yourself to a Super Bath"—contains advice that will help you turn your master bath into a well-outfitted dressing room, a place for a hot tub, garden room, or even a full-fledged exercise center (see pages 120 and 121 for more about this).

You don't, however, need a palace-size bath to make it do more. The one *at right* isn't overly large, yet its fireplace transforms the room by setting up a pleasant contrast to the bath's sleek, glossy surfaces.

Furnishings in a master bath should be adapted to your plans for using the room. Add a love seat or chaise longue, for instance, when the space is doubling as a place to get away from it all.

Good lighting is also a must. Wardrobe closets, makeup centers, and reading areas all require specialized lighting. Pages 40 and 41 provide helpful illuminating tips.

Before you begin building your dream, though, remember that even in a multipurpose room, you should be able to use the bath facilities—comfortably—without other things getting in the way.

DO YOUR BATHS HAVE A DATED LOOK?

If your bath is structurally sound but looks as though the years have passed it by, try giving the room new life, without sacrificing its old-fashioned appeal. Save vintage fixtures and fittings—or replace them with updated versions—and turn your remodeler's eye to the rest of the room. With a little ingenuity, you can revitalize a washed-up bath and turn it into a real bathing beauty.

Instead of apologizing for old-fashioned bath fixtures—a claw-foot tub or pedestal lavatory, for example—search for ways to play up their character. (Pages 32-33 and 38-39 describe decorating schemes that work.) For example, consider how they would look surrounded by modern surfaces. You can update your bath just by introducing fresh wall and floor coverings made from wood, tile, brick, or laminate, to name several. Chapter 3—"Bathroom Surfaces Make a Material Difference"—provides detailed help in choosing those that are right for your room.

The bath *opposite* (before) and *at right* (after) sparkled back to life with new, yet traditional, surface treatments—paneling and a vinyl wall covering. The handsome molding midway up the wall is a holdover from the old days.

If you don't want *too* much of the old look, think about boxing in fixtures, as the owner did here. Pages 34 and 35 offer decorating tips to help you out, and pages 126 and 127 discuss specific solutions you can adapt to your own bath.

Choosing vintage fixtures requires careful shopping. (See pages 88 and 89 to find out where to look and what to look out for.) If you can't find any that work—don't give up. Most plumbing-ware manufacturers market reproductions that are both charmingly old-fashioned and reliably modern.

WHAT
COULD NEW
FIXTURES DO?

Are you satisfied with the way your bathroom works but tired of the way it looks? If you answered "yes," maybe it's time to install new plumbing fixtures—they can bring out the best in any bath. Lavatories, tubs, showers, toilets, and bidets come in an eye-popping array of colors and styles to suit every decorating theme.

For a bath to work well, you need space, light, and plumbing fixtures that do their job. For it to look good, too, those plumbing fixtures must be compatible with the design scheme.

Remodeling a bath is one way to get the "pulled together" look. When you start from scratch, you have a chance to make the room exactly the way you want it. Chapter 6—"How to Add or Remodel a Bath"—takes you step by step through the process.

A less expensive and less time-consuming alternative is to replace the plumbing fixtures only. As Chapter 5—"Selecting Bathroom Components"—makes clear, they come in a wide range of sizes, shapes, designs, and colors.

Imagine what colorful new fixtures could do for your bath. *At left,* sleek, streamlined, cobalt-blue fixtures play against a bright white background to create a stunning visual effect. The handsome imports include a circular, see-through shower stall and a freestanding storage tower that separate the grooming area from the bidet and toilet.

Also, consider less conventional fixtures that can turn your bath into a great place to be. Platform tubs, sunken tubs, hot tubs, whirlpools, and saunas are all satisfying and useful additions. Chapter 7—"Treat Yourself to a Super Bath"—describes what you should know about each.

If new fixtures are out of the question, you can get splendid results by reinvigorating those you have. For example, an old piece of furniture, fitted with a lavatory, makes a one-of-a-kind washstand. Chapter 8—"Bathroom Projects You Can Build"—contains similarly imaginative suggestions on how to perk up your bath.

WHERE CAN YOU FIND ROOM FOR A NEW BATH?

If your family is growing, you may need another bath. Start searching for space by examining all the nooks and crannies in your house. If you find a small spot that's not being used, you may have the beginnings of a new bathroom.

If your bathroom resembles Grand Central Station at rush hour, it's time to plan a new one. First, figure out when your bath is most crowded and what's causing the congestion. Then look for room you can expand into. Often, a half bath near the family room can take the load off a one-bath house, as can a secondary bath with a shower stall located in the basement. Pages 74 and 75 present ways to squeeze a half bath into existing space.

Also, evaluate areas close to the bedrooms. A vacant corner of the master bedroom is a likely spot for an additional bath. Similarly, a seldom-used closet, when expanded, can easily become a full bath.

Look for well-hidden spaces. This sumptuous bath and adjoining bedroom *opposite* and *above* were carved out of space in the attic.

If you can't find extra room, consider an addition to your house. A simple extension under a roof overhang may yield enough space for a full bath.

Pages 76 and 77 examine the ins and outs of adding on.

Obviously, there are many different ways to arrange a new bath and different places to put it. On pages 155-157 are fixture templates showing workable sizes and fixture configurations. Use these aids and the advice in Chapter 4—"Getting a New Bath on Paper"—to pinpoint the best spot in your house. Once you've taken this step, read Chapter 6—"How to Add or Remodel a Bath."

WOULD YOUR FAMILY ENJOY AN AT-HOME SPA?

A century ago it was fashionable to "take the waters" at resorts built around mineral springs. Today, you can take the waters at home by settling into a sauna, steam bath, hot tub, or soaking tub. Mass production and do-it-yourself kits have caused sky-high prices to drop dramatically, so these one-time luxuries are now within reach of many family budgets.

One of the beauties of an at-home spa is that it needn't even be *in* your home, as the photo *at right* demonstrates. Sunk into a secluded deck, this hot tub adds the allurements of nature to the therapeutic benefits of a refreshing soak.

All spas should be located in a place where you can enjoy them easily and conveniently. After all, if you have to walk through the living area of your house in workout clothes or a swimsuit to reach the tub, you'll be less likely to use it. An area in or adjacent to the master bedroom/bath is ideal for any kind of spa. (If you decide on an outside location, consider whether wind, clouds, and cold will limit the times you can use the facility.) Inside, of course, you must cope with heat and moisture. Chapter 7— "Treat Yourself to a Super Bath"— discusses how to set up a variety of at-home spas.

Saunas, for example, must be closed off from other spaces, but hot tubs and soaking tubs can be out in the open. In addition, plans for a new bath can be adjusted to include a spa or even an exercise center. Pages 120 and 121 describe space requirements for major exercise equipment.

If, however, floor space is at a premium, you'll find many accessories that can turn an ordinary bath into an extraordinary place to be. Chapter 9—"Stocking Your Bath"— analyzes dozens of people-pampering products you can use.

CAN YOU "SOLARIZE" TO BUILD A BATH THAT HEATS ITSELF?

If your bath has the right exterior exposure, you may be able to "solarize" it by transforming it into a working sunspace. Any warmth you gain from the sun allows you to use your conventional heating system less, which translates to lower energy bills. If you also can use the sun to heat or preheat your water, you'll save even more money.

For a room to work using warmth from the sun, it must be designed to do three jobs: collect, store, and control solar heat. The bath shown here does all of them well. Fiber-glass panels collect the heat, quarry tile floors store it, and operable windows control its distribution.

To benefit from solarizing, a bath should face at least partially south. Here, south-facing, translucent panels draw in a lot of warmth even during the winter. Double- or triple-pane windows could also act as collectors. Clear glass, however, may compromise your privacy. Pages 44 through 47 contain ideas on how to shut out the world, while still letting the sun shine in.

At night, bathroom sunspaces shouldn't go into a deep freeze. With proper heat storage, they won't. Quarry tile, masonry floors and walls, and tanks of water all can gather heat during the day and then radiate it into the room after dark.

Other ways to control the distribution of solar heat include circulating fans, venting skylights, operable sashes, and exhaust units.

One special option is using a solar water-heating device to make a bath even more energy efficient. So much hot water is needed, it often makes sense to install a solar heater near where the hot water is being used.

Finally, in any solarization, it's usually a good idea to consult an architect or other design professional.

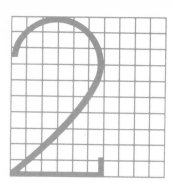

GIVE YOUR BATH A FRESH LOOK

Whether you're tired of the bathroom you have or you feel it's just time for a change, there are many ways to make a bathroom look different—and better—than it did before. Try enlivening walls and ceilings. Or make a big bath cozier. Fix up old fixtures. Or install a vanity. The point is, no bath is beyond help. What you need are inspiration and ideas. Read on for both.

DRESS THE WALLS WITH COLOR AND TEXTURE

When you look objectively at a bath and its design components, you come face-to-face with the truth. The room is more than 50 percent hard, shiny surfaces. And even though those cold, slick items—tub, toilet, tile walls, and floor—are necessary or practical, they aren't always the most decorative. So how *do* you offset all the austere porcelain and ceramic surfaces? Take to the walls with interesting textures and appealing colors.

The color connection

One pleasing color used on walls and in towels and accessories ties the whole bath together visually. It connects all the available design elements and effectively warms up the cold, hard surfaces. For example, the bright yellow in the bath *opposite, top* plays down the big white porcelain tub and tile backsplash. In fact, the sunshine color bounces off the shiny white surfaces, giving the whole room a soft, warm glow.

If your bath has few windows and little natural light, choose a bright, warm color (yellow, orange, copper-tinged browns, or shades of red) to lighten and brighten the area. And remember, light colors make a room look larger; darker, more intense colors make a room look smaller and cozier. By picking the right color and its most flattering value, you can play all the visual tricks a designer does.

If you paint the walls to add color, choose a good grade of enamel. A gloss or semigloss surface will wipe clean easily and give you years of service.

Existing tile walls shouldn't stop you from adding a new color to the bath. Check with your dealer for epoxy paints that let you change the color of tile easily without worrying about peeling.

If you're using wall coverings to add color, be sure you choose a good grade of vinyl that's impervious to moisture and can be cleaned easily.

Rough it up

Contrast is the designer's spice of life. One surface of color placed so it contrasts with another nearby creates visual excitement, like the kind at work in the bathroom *opposite, bottom*. Rugged, rough-textured boards contrast with the white porcelain fixtures and white laminate counter top. The result is that the wood looks more textured and the counter top more pristine because of their relationship to each other.

To balance enormous areas of porcelain fixtures or tiles in your bath, nothing gets the job done faster or more effectively than texture. And adding texture to walls is a good way to make them come to life again. Use heavily textured vinyl wall covering, brick or stone veneer, or, as in the bath *opposite, bottom*, rough-sawn boards. Several less obvious choices can yield equally interesting results. Try applying carpet to bathroom walls for texture, softness, sound control, and warmth. Use exterior siding or shake shingles for other unusual effects.

ADD A
VANITY

Anyone who has balanced toothpaste, brush, and glass on the edge of a wash basin knows the value of a vanity—it's practical. From the standpoint of design, a vanity is just as important. In addition to being a larger, more impressive element in your bath, a vanity provides a customized feature to an otherwise standard fixture—the lavatory basin. At the same time, adding a vanity to your bath gives you a chance to repeat existing colors and textures or introduce new ones.

mulated in the bathroom, you might use space under the top of the vanity for laundry bins. If so, plan proper ventilation so damp towels or garments don't mildew.

Add style

As a built-in accent, a vanity will stand out if you finish it in a color or material that contrasts with the wall surrounding it. Notice how the clean-lined, white laminated plastic vanity *at left* plays off the natural wood of the walls.

On the other hand, if you want the vanity to perform all its functions as inconspicuously as possible, finish it in colors or materials that blend with the background of the area. The vanity *opposite* shows you how. Its dark counter top is edged with the same 1x10 cedar board as that used for the bath's vertical surfaces.

A small vanity will look more impressive if all its surfaces are the same color and material. A larger vanity, however, can have a contrasting top without looking out of place.

If the vanity features an accent color, make sure the same color appears in other areas of the bath—in towels, shower curtain, wall pieces, or other accessories. The repetition of color helps to establish an ordered, well-decorated look.

U sually, even a small bath can accommodate a vanity. With a little ingenuity, you can use the room's need for a lavatory as a reason for adding counter space, storage, and a bit of extra glamour to your bath.

Add counter space

Don't limit the top of a vanity to the inches surrounding the lavatory. It can easily span the whole lavatory wall, like the one in the bath *opposite*. Here, the vanity counter tapers to shelf proportions over the raised "drying-off" area adja-

cent to this bath's shower. You could do the same thing with a handy shelf above a bathtub or toilet.

The surface you use for the top of the vanity is important. Choose a material that cleans easily and can't be damaged by water, bath products, or cosmetics. One common material is laminated plastic, available in an array of colors, including new high-style deep tones, wood grains, or a slate pattern that simulates the texture of the real thing.

Other choices to consider are ceramic tile, marble, manmade marble, or natural wood sealed with several coats of polyurethane to make it impervious to moisture.

Add storage space

A vanity can be more than a frame for your lavatory—more, even, than additional counter space. Through careful planning, you can convert previously wasted space into precious storage. The vanity in the bath *above*, for example, complements the two lavatories with tilt-top storage compartments perfect for cosmetics and grooming aids. Or, if you wish, you can equip the space between the vanity counter and floor with pullout drawers or shelves tucked behind cabinet doors.

Because much of a household's soiled clothing is accu-

BRIGHTEN THE CEILING

If you have a dim view of the way your bathroom looks, try brightening the ceiling. With new lights on the subject, you'll be able to see things more clearly in an even, shadow-free environment. At the same time, if your bathroom is too small, the right light can make it look larger than it is. In addition, the source of light—whether natural or artificial—can often be an important design element.

New lighting fixtures will do much to brighten a dim bathroom. Depending on the size and architecture of your bath, you can increase the amount of light in one of two ways.

Natural light

A skylight not only lets the sun shine in, it visually opens up the room, making it seem larger than it really is. The remodelers of the bath *opposite* took advantage of an angled ceiling to install a bank of windows over the platformed tub. If you add slanted skylights facing south, you also can give your home a passive solar boost—and a buffer to inflationary heating costs.

You might want to try prefab skylights in an upstairs bathroom; in other situations, you could install regular windows in the configuration that works best for the room.

Artificial light

When natural light is not available, you can get many of the same benefits with artificial light. The bath *at left* features a lighted ceiling surfaced with translucent plastic panels. If you like, use stained-glass panels in a lighted ceiling; the panels then become a decorating focal point.

Although the skylights provide major daytime lighting in the bath *opposite,* track lights mounted near them provide spot lighting after dark.

Achieve a similarly bright effect by installing a series of multi-bulb strip lights across the ceiling.

Finally, use reflected light, as well. A highly reflective surface will heighten and brighten the ceiling of your bath. Choose mirror tiles, Mylar, foil wall covering, or lacquer.

CUSTOMIZE WITH ANTIQUES

Thanks to energetic nostalgia buffs, wrecking crews have stopped destroying wonderful old pedestal lavatories and claw-foot bathtubs. Antiques of all kinds are now choice finds for home decorators. And with good reason. These bits of antiquity can add unique charm to a nondescript bath. (If your bathroom already has old-timey fixtures, see pages 36 and 37 for information about how to play them up in a new way.)

Baths can be "antiquated" in two ways. There are those antiques that come with the territory—such as the interesting old tiles, fixtures, and windows found in many vintage houses. And then there are the antiques you transplant into more modern surroundings. Either variety—or both—puts your individual hallmark on a bath.

Transplanting the past

The bath *opposite* is an antique haven. It was already blessed with the pedestal lavatory, but everything else was added. In this case, the antique environment is given a further boost by the Art Nouveau armoire, with its sinuous lines, beveled mirror, and delicately leaded glass door panel.

Of course, what you bring into your bath depends on what was there to begin with and what result you have in mind. In some cases, you may want to transplant an antique lavatory or window panel, as was done in the bath *at right.* In it, an old-fashioned sink has been set into a white laminated plastic backing and helps to add a touch of charm to a less-than-antique house. (For more on how to select antique plumbing fixtures, see pages 88 and 89.)

Plan present-day function

Although antiques can get by on their looks alone, your bath needs something more. It can appear to be a product of the gaslight and pull-chain toilet era, but it has to function with up-to-date convenience. So make sure the wiring and plumbing are modern, and all surfaces are practical and easy to clean. Then, add the charm and flavor of antiques in furnishings, accessories, and other decorative items.

BOX IN FIXTURES

Tired of looking at—and cleaning—the underpinnings of an ungainly old sink or claw-foot tub? Maybe all that's needed is some repackaging—in a wood, tile, or carpeted box. New fixtures, like the tub shown on the opposite page, can also benefit from the box trick.

Boxing in a bathroom fixture might be the best way to go—not only can you hide an old fixture or set off a new one, but you may also use the box itself as extra storage or counter space.

Old fixtures look new
In many homes, an old high-backed sink like the one *above* is a common feature. This one, however, takes on a whole new look with a trim pine cabinet surrounding it. The white laminated plastic top provides a spacious mar-gin around the rim of the sink and alters the proportions of the unit just enough to give it a more modern look. An old-fashioned tub could easily receive the same treatment. When planning the project, don't box yourself into a corner by cutting off access to the plumbing. Make sure you can reach it easily.

New fixtures look even better
Like their older counterparts, sparkling new fixtures can sometimes benefit from a cus-tomizing treatment. The blue whirlpool tub *opposite* is a good example. The tile surrounding it not only sets up an easy step into the tub, it also makes the new whirlpool a focal point for the decorating scheme.

Before beginning to box in fixtures, remember, they're in a bathroom. Choose materials that are impervious to moisture, with surfaces that can stand up to accidental spills of bath products or cosmetics. (More about boxing in fixtures on pages 126 and 127.)

GIVE YOUR BATH A FRESH LOOK

PLAY UP INTERESTING FIXTURES

Not all old fixtures deserve to be hidden behind boxes. Pedestal-style lavatories, tubs-on-legs, even old-fashioned toilets, are often glamorous enough to play major roles in a decorating scheme. The choice is yours, of course, but if you want to emphasize the antiquity in your bath, here's how to do it.

Before you decide to play up a fixture, determine whether it truly has intrinsic interest. Look for graceful, curving lines, relief work, wood or brass details, or other features not normally seen in modern baths. Many early ceramic designs were produced in limited numbers by artisans who brought sculptural qualities to everyday items. Humbler, porcelain-on-iron fixtures were more common, but also offer nostalgic appeal.

Restoration and reclamation

A fixture in less than mint condition can be given a second chance at life. Look in your Yellow Pages for porcelain glazing firms that resurface old fixtures. If the unit is in good condition but the porcelain is stained, you may be able to remove the stains, as explained on page 145.

You can buy faucets and fittings from companies specializing in reproductions of antique hardware, in addition to electrical and plumbing items. The same firms also have reproduction towel bars, soap holders, and other vintage bath accessories.

Fixtures as a focal point

Fixtures that rate a second look deserve to play a key role in your decorating scheme. And the best way to give fixtures the attention they merit is to contrast them with other decorating elements.

Color is one way to do it. The sparkling white bath fixture *at left,* for instance, contrasts sharply with a dark, forest green wall and deep-toned tiled floor.

Any dark or bright color will create the same effect. On the other hand, a light or white background provides no contrast for the fixtures and would make them less obvious and less interesting.

Shape is another design element you can use to give focus to your fixtures. The ornate shape of old lavatories and tubs shows up to better advantage if the background of the bath is simple and without pattern. A wall covering with a strong design would soften the silhouette of the fixtures, causing them to blend into the background and lose some of their unique character.

Style is a third way to provide contrast. By introducing a few sleek-lined, contemporary pieces into the bath, you play the new off the old, making them both more pleasingly attractive.

Fixtures as style-setters

In many cases, old fixtures are just the beginning of an entire decorating scheme. The bath shown *at left* belongs to lovers of Victoriana, so the feeling of the era extends well beyond the fixtures. An antique washstand, with bowl and pitcher, fills the corner, while a cabinet displaying antique collectibles lines one wall. Even though the wall-mounted lights are new, the homeowners found antique shades to make the lighting fixtures conform with the rest of the bath's decor.

If you're building an entire bath around old fixtures, use fabrics, patterns, wall art, hardware, and other accessories to reinforce the mood or style you're creating.

GIVE YOUR BATH A FRESH LOOK

RELAX WITH GREENERY

One sure way to soften the antiseptic, hospital-like quality of cool bathroom surfaces is to use them as a backdrop for green, growing things. What are the two key elements any plant needs to thrive? And which plants do especially well in bathroom environments? Here are some answers.

Your bathroom's naturally high humidity means nearly any plant can get all the moisture it needs (though regular watering is still necessary). Light, however, is equally important to the greening of a bathroom. And in a bathroom, getting the right light is usually the bigger problem.

Levels of light
Whether the light source is natural or artificial, most plants require one of three intensities: direct sunlight; a bright indirect light (sometimes referred to as diffused, filtered, or curtain sunlight); or a low-level light that approximates outdoor shade.

A skylight or large window as shown *opposite* is probably the only way you'll provide direct sunlight in a bathroom. A window facing east or west will give you plenty of medium, indirect light; however, if your bath has only a small window and your plants need a lot of sun, plan to help them out by putting them under grow lights for at least 10 to 14 hours a day.

Whatever your situation, the day's normal patterns—when family members turn bathroom lights on, then quickly snap them off—will *not* provide enough light for healthy plant growth.

Plant places
Where to plant your plants is an important question. If you have plenty of floor space, you'll have no problem displaying an indoor tree. Use a counter or shelf for tabletop plants. Or take to the ceiling, instead. Hanging plants admirably decorate otherwise unused space.

Indoor trees
Here are adaptable floor-standing plants that will do well in your bath:
● *Areca palm* likes bright, indirect sunlight.
● *Dieffenbachia* tolerates light ranging from poor to bright, indirect.
● *Dracaena marginata* needs bright, indirect light.
● *Ficus benjamina* or weeping fig prefers bright, indirect light.
● *Ficus elastica* or rubber plant requires the same light as the weeping fig.

Counter-top varieties
● *Piggyback* likes bright, indirect light.
● *Peperomia* prefers medium light, no direct sun.
● *Chinese evergreen* tolerates low light levels, does not require bright light.
● *Coleus* thrives in direct sunlight or bright light.
● *Jade plant* needs direct sunlight or bright, indirect light.

Hanging plants
● *Wandering Jew* will grow in low-level light but is more colorful in brighter light.
● *Asparagus fern* prefers part shade or filtered light.
● *Swedish ivy* thrives in bright, indirect light.
● *German ivy* prefers low light conditions.
● *Boston fern* does well under bright, indirect or filtered light.
● *Airplane plant* or spider plant loves bright light but no direct sunlight.
● *Grape ivy* tolerates low light conditions.
● *English ivy* will grow well in low light.

GOOD LIGHTING LETS YOU GET A GOOD LOOK AT YOURSELF

The bathroom is no place to be in the dark. Especially early in the morning—or late at night—when your sleepy head needs all the help it can get. Good light won't wake you up right away, but it will make using a razor or stroking on eye shadow less hazardous. At the same time, the right choice of light levels and fixtures lets the natural beauty of your bathroom shine through.

If you're going to see yourself as you truly are, lighting in the bathroom must be efficient and well-placed. You need enough light—and from three directions—to really get a good look at yourself.

Where the light falls

Focus the light on the area around your mirror and lavatory. The most efficient lighting for shaving or putting on makeup comes from three directions: a 75-watt light on either side of your face and a 100- to 150-watt light above the mirror. The top light usually bounces off a light-colored basin below so a shaver can clearly see the underside of his chin.

With a basin-sized mirror, the best location for side lights is 15 inches to either side of the mirror's center. At these distances, plan 40 watts of incandescent or 20 watts of fluorescent lighting for each side. However, if your lavatory is topped by a large expanse of mirror, you'll have to stretch the dimensions. The farther from the center of the mirror they are, the more wattage each fixture should have. That way, the light is as bright as it would be if the fixtures were closer to your face. Light a bathroom mirror with soft white bulbs or fluorescent tubes in "natural white" or "deluxe warm white"; these are the most flattering to skin tones. And avoid backlighting. A light shining from behind makes it difficult to look into the mirror in front of you.

How to light up a bath

Finding the right light is relatively easy because there are so many different light fixtures. Some mirror units come with side lights, top lights, or both. Another option is the multi-bulbed strip lighting you can

buy in various lengths and install around the mirror, like those pictured in the bathroom *opposite*. Achieve the same effect with fluorescent tubes or use a series of separate light fixtures, like the arrangement in the bathroom *above*. (Energy-efficient fluorescents give off three to five times as much light as incandescent bulbs. Warm-toned tubes give off light that blends well with bulb light.)

Light, more light

To make your bathroom even brighter, add reflective surfaces. Light bounced off a mirror increases in intensity. Reflective surfaces on walls and ceiling also lift the light level. In the bath *above* foil wall covering reflects light, as does the white and brushed-aluminum vanity.

GIVE YOUR BATH A FRESH LOOK

MAKE A BIG BATH COZIER

Large baths may not be big bargains. Some of them—especially those that once were bedrooms in older homes (with plumbing added later)—contain too much space to be comfortable. Most of us expect bathrooms to be smaller, more personal, and more efficient. If your bath is the size of a stateroom on a luxury liner, think small. Here are some tips on how to decorate it down to a more intimate scale.

Making a big bath cozy means making it *look* smaller. One of the dozen tips described below should get the job done.

Reduce the visual size
Try one of these suggestions to make a big bathroom seem more intimate.
• Use a dark or bright color to visually bring the walls closer.
• Use a patterned wall covering. The bolder the pattern, the more an overly large space will seem to shrink visually.
• Use color (preferably dark or bright) on the ceiling and floor. Color creates an effect of bringing the two surfaces closer together, snugging up the room's visual proportions.

Fill excess space
Objects take up space, cutting a big room down to size. Here are a few space-filling suggestions for your bath.
• Add furniture to fill bare walls or vacant corners. The larger the bath, the larger the scale or size of the furniture should be. Everything from towel racks to armoires, from chaises to porch furniture can become practical additions to a bath, while filling those wide open spaces.
• Add plants. Floor-standing or hanging plants take up space and bring a fresh, lively look to your bath at the same time. (For 18 plants that grow well in bathrooms, see page 38.)
• Hang things. Undecorated walls, austere and exposed, make any bath look larger. Cover them with oversized weavings, tapestries, framed posters, bits of architecture, or anything, in fact, that's interesting to look at. (Care

should be taken when hanging anything in a moist environment. Be sure proper ventilation exists.)

Give the area charm
The bath *at right* gives you an idea of just how cozy a big, old bath can be. A spindle towel bar and an old dry sink outfitted with a new lavatory occupy some of the excess space. The floor is dark wood with a polyurethane protective covering, and the walls are dressed in dark paper with a tiny overall pattern.
Some other tips for your bath:
• Use inviting colors that come from the warm side of the color wheel (red, orange, yellow).
• Use a wall covering with a quaint pattern. Small geometrics, patchwork patterns, or miniature florals give the cozy feeling you're after.
• Try soft textures. A plush carpet and fluffy towels will take the hard edges off a big bathroom. Use flocked wall covering or textured walls instead of sleek wall finishes like lacquer, mirror, or tile. And don't be afraid to cover the walls with carpet. It can soften your bath in a big way. (Again, keep soft textures—especially flocked wall coverings—away from high-humidity zones such as showers.)
• Select warm, time-worn wood.
• Use plenty of mood-setting accessories to accent the walls, counter tops, or floor. Antique or reproduction towel bars, hooks, or hardware are good bets.
• Bathe the room in warm light. If you have fluorescent lighting, use only warm-white tubes. Pink incandescent bulbs or shaded light fixtures also create a softer look.

CREATE PRIVACY WITH WINDOW TREATMENTS

In a bathroom, windows don't make good neighbors. To gain privacy, you'll have to shield all that glass with a window treatment. The best cover-up allows you to see out when you want to and let in light when you need to—all without sacrificing the sense of seclusion any good bathroom should have.

Seeing out a window without being seen is a special problem. The window treatments in both baths pictured here have solved it. The shutters in the bath *opposite* and the mini-blinds in the one *at left* are adjustable; they allow light to enter the room without compromising your privacy. The adjustable louvers or slats also permit a glimpse of the outside world in complete privacy.

The shuttered window even lets you choose how much privacy you want. If you need more light, just keep the top shutters open.

Letting in light

If privacy is your prime objective, try using curtains, draperies, Roman shades of opaque fabric, roll shades, or shades of woven wood. On the other hand, if you want to let in as much light as possible—and still retain your privacy—different window treatments will do the job better.

For example, gather a flat panel of semisheer fabric, top and bottom, on tension rods mounted inside the bathroom window casing. Or, in a more formally decorated room, hang a gossamer Austrian shade at the window.

If fabric isn't for you, try another transparent solution. Replace or cover the existing window with a stained-glass panel or a piece of frosted glass or translucent plastic. If you're remodeling a bath or building a new home, consider using translucent glass block. It will let the light shine in on a securely private bath.

45

OTHER WAYS TO PROVIDE PRIVACY

If you live in splendid isolation, taking a private bath is as easy and peaceful as stepping into the tub and relaxing luxuriously. But if a congested urban or suburban area is home, ensuring your privacy is sometimes more difficult to do. To keep the outside world where it belongs, you may need a clever privacy screen.

A picture window beside your bathtub? It's possible—if you follow the plan used by the owners of the bath *above*. They replaced the usual tiled tub wall with a plate glass panel, ¼ inch thick. Then outside the window, they constructed a lattice-roofed "greenhouse." Finally, to ensure complete privacy, they mounted translucent plastic panels between the 2x4 framing members.

A less tropical approach
The bath *opposite* is another open-to-the-world area, though this house, unlike the one described above, is in a cooler climate. Located on the top floor, the bathroom has a skylight with a relaxing view of the tree tops. Frosted panels create the needed privacy.

If you have the option of installing glass wherever you want it, you can have plenty of light and still maintain complete privacy. A skylight, similar to the one shown *opposite*, is one way to go. Another is a series of clerestory windows high on the bath wall.

If the windows in your bathroom don't offer much privacy, try another suggestion. Install a prefab, bump-out greenhouse loaded with light-filtering, view-blocking plants. The visual effect is similar to the one produced by the bath *above*, but on a much smaller scale and with access to the plants from inside the bath.

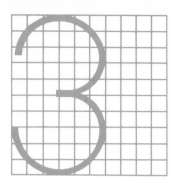

BATHROOM SURFACES MAKE A MATERIAL DIFFERENCE

When it comes to maintaining your bath, you must stay on top of things. Old, worn surfaces not only look bad, they also may leak, trap odors, and prove stubbornly hard to clean. Walls, floors, tub surrounds, and counters all lend themselves to relatively inexpensive, but attractive, makeovers. This chapter examines the best ways to transform bathroom surfaces and describes—in handy chart form—the strengths and weaknesses of common materials you may use.

Appearances aren't deceiving; they tell a lot about your bath—how well it works and what changes are needed most. The quickest way to transform a bath is to change the look of its walls. The photographs *opposite* depict four common face-lifts—using paint, a wall covering, paneling, and tile.

Whatever materials you choose, they, like the ones here, must stand up to water, steam, heat, and a whole lot of cleaning.

Paint

The painted cornflower blue wall *opposite, upper left* is a real eye-opener. Though painting a wall may be the easiest way to redecorate, you'll need a patient, steady hand when cutting in paint around fixtures and cabinets.

Tough gloss and semigloss paints work best in a humid bath. However, they must be applied to a smooth surface—glossier paints exaggerate all the lumps and bumps on a wall. In addition, glossy surfaces are easier to clean than flat finishes, and because moisture doesn't get to them as easily, they can take repeated washings.

Vinyl wall coverings

Wall coverings are another popular choice. They're a terrific way to introduce pattern and color to a small space. Ordinary wallpaper, of course, is not the answer in most baths; it's hard to clean and doesn't resist moisture very well. Vinyl, plastic-coated, or foil wall coverings—like the one *opposite, center left*—are the best materials. They clean easily and stand up to a damp rag and mild detergent. Remember one thing: Any wall covering in a bath must be able to take the heat and humidity.

Wood

Wood is more expensive than paint or wall coverings. But it gives a look and feel like no other material—mellow, warm, cozy, and natural.

You can select paneling from a wide variety of hardboards made to look like wood (or other materials), natural wood veneers, and wood planks, like the ones applied horizontally to the bath wall *opposite, upper right*. Any bathroom surface made of real wood must be sealed so it won't soak up moisture and accumulate dirt.

Tile

Ceramic tile has it all—it's beautiful, it won't fade or stain, and it's *waterproof*, unlike other materials, which are water-resistant. True, it's also expensive, but tile is usually worth the money: Properly installed, it should last a lifetime.

Smaller mosaic tiles, like the ones in the photograph *opposite, below,* come bonded to pieces of 1x1- or 1x2-foot paper or mesh; they go up a bit faster than the larger sizes, but require more grouting.

Mirror tiles can make a small powder room or bath look bigger. Keep in mind, however, that the silver mirror backing disintegrates when it becomes permanently damp. In especially wet areas of the bath, use acrylic mirror tiles to achieve the same effect.

(continued)

BATHROOM
SURFACES
MAKE A
MATERIAL
DIFFERENCE

WALLS
(continued)

YOUR WALL OPTIONS

EFFECTS

PAINT
Latex
Alkyd
Urethane
Polyurethane
Epoxy

Colors come in a wide range of hues; many are standard, but almost any paint can be mixed to your liking. Finishes range from flat to high gloss, but a medium-gloss finish is most suitable for bathroom walls. Additives allow you to texture the paint so it resembles a plastered surface.

VINYL
Paper-backed vinyl
Cloth-backed vinyl
Wet-look vinyl
Foil

Wall coverings that work well in a bath can be found in a style to suit every taste. The many colors, patterns, and textures help make them the most popular choice for bathroom walls. Some kinds come already pasted with an adhesive coating that only needs to be dampened to adhere to the wall; others can be stripped from the wall without steaming or scraping. All wall coverings in a bath should resist moisture and be able to take a scrubbing.

PANELING
Plywood
Hardboard
Solid planks
Plastic laminate

Natural wood—or something made to look like it—warms up a bath like no other material can. Printed hardboards are available in many colors and designs, including wood grains. Veneers backed by plywood—commonly called paneling—are popular ways to dress up a bath, as are planks like barnboards and tongue-and-groove boards. In addition, plastic laminates can imitate the look of grass cloth, marble, even fine wood; they also come in plain, solidly colored sheets, and geometric patterns.

TILE
Ceramic tile
Mosaic tile
Mirror tile

Tiles come glazed and unglazed, plain and patterned, in just about any color you want. You can also buy hand-painted tiles and design your own patterns. Usually, tiles are 4¼ or 6 inches square, but there are many other sizes and shapes to choose from. To make cleaning easier, wall tiles are ordinarily glossier than floor tiles.

DURABILITY	USES	INSTALLATION	COSTS
The higher the gloss, the easier the surface is to maintain. Usually semigloss works best, because it won't collect condensation as much as the glossier paints. Epoxy and urethane stand up to the toughest wear.	Apply latex and alkyd to primed or previously painted surfaces. When switching from latex to alkyd, a primer is needed. Urethanes adhere to most walls. Save epoxy paints for tile, glass, and porcelain surfaces.	One gallon usually covers about 400 square feet. Latex is the simplest to work with; alkyd, a touch more difficult. Epoxy is the most difficult to mix and apply.	Latex is usually the least expensive, followed by alkyd and urethanes. Epoxy is the most expensive. Regardless of type, deeper colors and shinier surfaces generally mean more expensive paints.
Stick with the vinyls; they stand up well to humidity. Those you can scrub are more practical and last longer. Steam rises; don't ask for trouble by papering the ceiling of this naturally humid spot.	Most wall coverings can be applied to a strong, clean surface. Strip or steam off old vinyl coverings first. To get a finished appearance, free of blemishes, use lining paper under wet-look vinyls and foils.	One roll typically covers 30 square feet. Widths vary from 20¼ to 28 inches. Pre-pasted coverings are easiest to install; foils, the most difficult.	Prices are quoted by the single roll, but wall coverings are generally sold only by the double roll. Prices vary widely. Foils are usually the most expensive; vinyls, moderate in cost.
Laminates are not affected by water; they also wipe clean easily. Hardboard is simpler to care for than real wood, which must be sealed with urethane or another water-resistant coating.	Perfect for covering up badly damaged, marred walls. Stop any leaks first. Use furring strips to get an even framework before applying. Use wood or metal molding, if desired, to hide joints.	Most paneling comes in 4x8-foot sheets. Some are installed with glue and nails; others, glue only. Laminate edges must be protected because moisture will warp the backing. Planks are available in various lengths and widths.	Printed hardboard is the least expensive; plywood and planks vary in cost depending on the type of wood being used. Laminates are moderately expensive, but newer patterns, finishes, and colors are making them more costly.
Waterproof and easy to care for when properly installed. Grout requires occasional cleaning to remove mildew and mold. Mirror tile joints are hard to waterproof; use where there won't be much moisture. Acrylic mirror tiles hold up better than glass in a bath.	Most tiles love water and are used anywhere in a bath. You can apply ceramic tiles to any drywall, plaster, or plywood surface that's smooth, sound, and firm. Unglazed tiles may need to be sealed.	Installing tile can be tricky. Measure with care; add 10 percent to allow for cutting and waste. Some kinds are available in sheets, with flexible grout already in place.	Ceramic and mosaic tiles may be luxuries. They are moderately to expensively priced, depending on size, color, and type. Other kinds are in a medium price range. Materials needed to install any tile increase the final cost.

FLOORS

Bathroom floors take a beating. In addition to bearing up underfoot, floors in the bath have to endure water and humidity day in and day out. Fortunately, most aren't defeated easily; they're built to take the wear and tear your family gives them.

Don't let choosing a floor for a bath get you down. When comparing different materials, ask and answer a number of questions. How does it look? Is it comfortable? Can you clean it easily? Does it cover up sounds or exaggerate them? Can you install the floor yourself, or do you need professional help? What does your budget say? No one floor covering is the right answer for all situations; but the three described below are the most popular and effective. The chart on pages 54 and 55 can help you match one floor covering to the needs of your own bath.

Carpeting

Carpeting *opposite, upper left* is warm and comfy to walk on, and, if installed correctly, it can look like a million dollars. On the other hand, carpeting retains moisture and gets dirty easily. As a general rule, carpets hold up best in powder rooms and master baths attached to bedrooms. In heavily traveled areas—especially if children are bouncing about—a hard-surface flooring is usually a better bet. Furthermore, it's not advisable to install permanent carpeting around bathroom fixtures. Simply lay loose carpeting around them, cleaning it whenever necessary.

Look for carpeting that will not retain odors, is mildew resistant, and is less susceptible to water soaking and staining.

Tile

Nothing is better looking or more versatile than tile. Glazed and unglazed tiles come in a kaleidoscope of colors, sizes, and shapes. (Quarry tiles, made of fired, unglazed clay, are available in earthy, natural colors; glazed ceramic tiles, in every color.) You can choose from ordinary stock tiles and create an extraordinary floor by setting them in an original pattern. The tile floor *opposite, upper right* is made of 4¼-inch squares and 6x4¼-inch rectangles, placed so no two rows end up alike. Black grout emphasizes the subtle horizontal and vertical lines.

Tiles are not as comfortable as resilient floors. They don't bounce pleasantly underfoot, and they're cold to the touch in the winter (but cool to the touch in the summer). In any event, all tile surfaces are tough, durable, and easy to care for.

Don't slip! Use tiles with slightly irregular surfaces and a non-gloss glaze on floors; save the high-gloss, wet-look, slippery tiles for counters and walls.

Installing most kinds of tile is best done by a professional because of the time and patience required to do the job properly. Pregrouted tiles or tiles mounted on sheets of mesh or paper are good candidates for the do-it-yourselfer.

Resilients

Resilient floors, as the name implies, are bouncy. They give slightly when you walk on them, but the surface is usually smooth and hard. They also feel warm to your feet—an important touch on cold winter mornings. Resilients can be installed over most other materials if the subfloors are smooth, solid, and sound. In addition,

you can choose the look you like: elegant marble, warm wood, sleek tile, or country brick like the bath *opposite, below*. To top it off, resilients are easy to care for.

• *Vinyl asbestos tile*—the least expensive of the resilients and the most popular—is a good choice for the bath. The tiles are sturdy and resist all kinds of potential damages—stains, burns, scuffing, and dents. Some even come with an adhesive back that makes installation easy.

• *Solid vinyl* is the most expensive resilient flooring, but it's also the most durable, though it's slightly vulnerable to burns. Solid vinyl comes in several grades and can be laid over an existing resilient floor covering. Generally, however, the work must be done by a professional.

• *Solid rubber tile*, until recently used only in industrial and commercial applications, is now appearing on the home front. Colors are clear, but they're muted and available in only a limited range of hues. Patterns (see page 54) feature raised circles and diamonds that make rubber tile more slip-resistant than other resilient materials. Installation is tricky and best left to professionals.

• *Cushioned sheet vinyl* is soft underfoot (it usually contains a layer of vinyl foam) and helps absorb sound—an important advantage if you're planning a children's bath. Several kinds are available, ranging in durability from that of vinyl asbestos tile to approximately one-half as durable. Cushioned-sheet vinyl is, however, vulnerable to burns.

(continued)

FLOORS
(continued)

YOUR FLOORING OPTIONS

EFFECTS

CARPET

Nylon
Polypropylene
Other

There is a color and texture to suit every decorating scheme. Wall to wall, carpeting creates a feeling of warmth; more practically, it *is* warm underfoot on chilly mornings. Carpeting also helps cut down on noise, but requires lots of care to look its best.

CERAMIC TILE

Glazed tile
Quarry tile

Some of the most exciting, high-fashion floors are covered with tile. You can choose from the typical 4¼- or 6-inch-square tiles, as well as mosaic and other sizes and shapes. Tiles come glazed or unglazed in a wide range of colors, designs, and textures. Grout also is colorfully varied.

RESILIENT

Vinyl asbestos tiles
Solid vinyl tiles
Rubber tiles
Sheet vinyl
Cushioned sheet vinyl

These comfortable-on-the-feet floor coverings come in a multitude of colors, textures, and finishes. However, you won't find many strong, clear colors, except in rubber and the solid vinyls. Most are muted, variegated, or patterned. Smooth and textured surfaces are available, as are cushioned-back resilients. You can find nearly any pattern—from marble and brick to Spanish tile and wood plank. Rubber tiles, shown *at left,* have a raised surface that improves traction.

DURABILITY	USES	INSTALLATION	COSTS
Choose carpeting that can stand moisture and resist mildew. Nylon and polypropylene wear well. To avoid stains, all spills must be wiped up promptly. Acrylic carpets are comfy on your feet, springy, and easy to clean. They also absorb sound well.	Warm and soft underfoot, carpets are a good choice for baths serving main living areas and adult-only powder rooms. Polypropylene is water-, insect-, and mold-resistant.	Roll goods are easily laid over any existing surface, except other carpeting, and are either laid loose or tacked in place. If moisture will soak through to the floor below, you will need a solid subfloor. Place nonskid pads or double-faced carpet adhesive tape under scatter rugs to prevent accidents.	All carpeting is sold by the square yard, or you may find a remnant that fits your bath. Prices range from inexpensive to moderately expensive, depending on fiber and backing. Modacrylic is the least expensive carpeting for use in a bathroom.
All tiles are exceptionally durable if they are properly installed. Grout is porous and requires regular cleaning. Quarry tile usually is not glazed, so it needs a stain-resistant sealer.	For beauty, luxury, and permanent performance, a tile floor is tops. There is a tile flooring suitable for every bath and decorating scheme.	Laying a tile floor is a feasible do-it-yourself project, but take care. Cutting, setting, and grouting require time, patience, and care. Pregrouted tiles are an easier way to get the same look. All tile must be installed on a completely level, unmarred subfloor.	Add up the cost of materials and installation, and you'll find this hard-surface flooring is the most expensive way to cover a bathroom floor.
High-grade solid vinyl is the most durable. No-wax surfaces make care simple—a damp mop restores the shiny finish. Except for rubber, other resilients require polish or wax. Rubber can be damaged by pertoleum-base products.	Correctly installed, resilients stand up to dirt and wear. They're good for children's baths and spots that serve as major clean-up areas.	Most resilient tiles are easy for the do-it-yourselfer to install; some even have a self-stick backing. Cushioned sheet vinyl is laid loose so most homeowners can handle putting it down. Leave other sheet goods and rubber tiles to a professional. Uneven floors may require plywood or hardboard underlayment.	Vinyl asbestos tiles are the most economical. Sheet goods vary in price depending on grade, pattern, and finish. Rubber, solid vinyl tiles, or sheet goods are moderate to expensive.

TUBS AND SHOWERS

When the family prefers showers and your baths have tubs that only suit soakers, adding another way to get wet is the way to go. There are three good methods to add a shower to your bath—one of them should be right for you.

In older bathrooms, tubs are the rub-a-dub norm. Even if there is a backsplash around the tub, it usually won't protect the wall from extensive water damage. Walls, whether they're plaster, drywall, or just insulation and studs, must be protected from moisture; therefore, the material you select for the tub-shower surrounds must be water*proof,* not just water-resistant. The chart on pages 58 and 59 summarizes information about the kind of material that may work best in your bath.

To bring things up-to-date in an older bath, consider adding a delightful shower. One of the methods mentioned here will keep everything else perfectly dry while you get pleasantly wet.

Plastic laminate
Smooth, colorful, and easy to care for, plastic laminate tub surrounds have a lot going for them.

If you've worked with laminate before, you won't have difficulty with shower surrounds like the one *opposite, left.* However, laminate can be tricky to work with. The panels must fit properly against the tub to prevent leaks, a job more difficult than it may seem. To make installation somewhat easier, kits are available with detailed instructions to show you how.

Laminate panels can go over any sound, smooth, level surface. Remove loose paint and any wall coverings. Previously untreated surfaces must have a moisture-resistant finish applied before the laminate panels go up. Laminate kits are made to fit the length of the existing tub; your job is to bond the laminate to the walls with laminate adhesive. To complete the job, you'll need to cut openings for faucets and

shower heads, using a hole saw or saber saw.

Fiber glass
Fiber-glass tub surrounds may be an all-encompassing solution to the problems in your bath. Many companies manufacture three- (and five-) piece units like the one *opposite, upper right* that would work well if you're planning to remodel a bath or add to it.

Fiber glass is a tough customer in the bath. It's waterproof, durable, and simple to clean. However, it's also easy to scratch with abrasive cleaners. Most manufacturers recommend that you clean fiber glass only with water, a mild dish detergent, or both.

Wall units are available in various sizes so fitting them isn't difficult if the walls are straight and true. The kits consist of two molded end panels and a center panel or panels. Installation is easy, but you do need to cut openings for fittings with a hole saw or saber saw. Adhesive comes with the kit, as does the caulking used to fill up all seams. (Fiber-glass and plastic surrounds come in several solid colors, with white one of the most popular.)

Tile
There are three reasons why tile has long been a favorite material to use in the bath: It's water-resistant, durable, and easy to care for. And because the adhesive not only holds the tiles in place but also acts as a moisture barrier, ceramic tiles are logical choices for the tub surrounds.

Colorful, stylish ceramic tiles are applied to any drywall, plaster, or plywood surface that's smooth, sound, and firm. Care must be taken, however, to ensure the adhesive will stick well to the surface. If you're resurfacing an area,

you'll need to strip off wallpaper or loose paint, or sand the sheen off glossy wall paint.

Mosaic tiles come bonded to sheets of 1x1- or 1x2-foot mesh or paper. These sheets go up faster than loose tiles, because you don't have to set each piece individually. Pre-grouted tile sheets in 4¼-inch-square tiles have flexible synthetic grouting. You stick the sheets to the wall first, then seal edges with a bead of caulking. Both kinds are sensible choices for the do-it-yourselfer: Installation is not as time-consuming as laying loose tile, nor does it require as much skill. On the other hand, mosaic tiles and pre-grouted sheets are available only in a limited choice of colors and styles.

Setting loose tile requires patience. The distance between each tile must be exactly the same. Spacers, available from tile dealers, help make this step easier. When the tile adhesive has set (it's a special kind used in high-moisture situations), grouting is then added.

While you're out shopping, price *all* the pieces of tile you'll need. Field tile (the flat 4¼- and 6-inch squares or other regular pieces) is much less expensive than the trim tiles you'll need. Sold by the linear foot, these necessary rounded, coved, and mitered pieces and caps can add substantially to the final cost of the job.

When ceramic tile is installed in a shower compartment like the one *opposite, lower right,* a shower floor membrane (receptor base) or floor pan must be installed below the tile to prevent leakage. (Typically, receptors are lead pans with sides about 4 inches high and include a drain outlet.)   *(continued)*

TUBS AND SHOWERS
(continued)

YOUR TUB AND SHOWER OPTIONS

EFFECTS

LAMINATE
Plastic laminate

Plastic laminate panels come in the same diverse range of colors, textures, and finishes used to make plastic laminate counter tops. In vertical applications, however, you can get by with $\frac{1}{32}$-inch-thick material, rather than the $\frac{1}{16}$-inch stock required for counters. Like other surrounds, laminate is simple to clean, won't leak easily, and is immune to mildew.

FIBER GLASS
Fiber glass
Acrylic
ABS plastic

Tub and shower surrounds add a sleek touch to the bath. Plus, they're great organizers: Soap trays, grab bars, and utility shelves are all part of one piece. Also, these molded units are never hot or cold to the touch; the material is inherently warm. Surrounds are available in white and a range of mostly pastel colors. Kits fit most standard tubs.

TILE
Ceramic tile

Ceramic tiles come in many sizes and shapes, the most common being 4¼- and 6-inch squares. Spaces with irregular dimensions can be easily tiled due to a wide variety of trim pieces available. Glazed tiles are impervious to soil and stains and are sold in a wide range of colors and patterns; some are painted by hand.

DURABILITY	USES	INSTALLATION	COSTS
Impervious to moisture when properly installed. Durable—but laminate can be scratched. Cleans easily with soap and water or mild detergent.	Ideal for all the watery spots in a bath.	Most homeowners can install plastic laminate without professional assistance; however, the sheets are so bulky another person must help hold the pieces in place. Install all panels on a smooth, dry surface. Cutouts for fittings need to be made during installation.	Moderately inexpensive to moderately expensive, depending on grade, color, and finish. But installing it yourself can save a bundle.
Water-resistant and moderately durable. Almost carefree surface: wipes clean with a damp cloth.	Three- to five-piece molded units are used in remodeling; they're made to be installed over existing standard-size, recessed tubs.	Precut panels are applied to solid walls with an adhesive. Panels come with pressure-sensitive tape that helps you hold pieces in place while adhesive sets. Joints in panels are caulked or filled to make the surrounds watertight. Kits contain detailed instructions.	Inexpensive to moderately expensive, depending on the grade, texture, and color. Won't bust many budgets because do-it-yourselfers can handle most or all of the work.
Water-resistant and durable when correctly installed. To prevent mildew and dirt from piling up, grout must be coated with a special sealer. A floor pan is a must below tile when installing a shower.	Tile wards off water like few other materials—excellent for floors, shower walls, and as a backsplash around the tub.	Use mastic to set tile on smooth, firm wall surfaces that are resistant to moisture. Putting up pregrouted tile is an alternative for the do-it-yourselfer with limited experience.	Moderately expensive but may be more costly if you're buying hand-decorated or imported tiles. Trim tiles are more expensive than field tiles. Installation by a professional adds significantly to the total bill.

COUNTERS

On the surface, bathroom counter tops must be tough. What other spot in the bath has to stand up to water, soap, alcohol- and acetone-based liquids, harsh cosmetics, and an array of abrasive tooth whiteners? If after years of use and abuse your counter top is showing its age, it may be time for a face-lift. And if your bath doesn't have a counter, it may be time to add one.

It might seem surprising to discover that you can replace a counter top without replacing the cabinet below it. If the existing surface is in good condition—smooth and sound—you can even lay new material right atop the old. In any case, removing the counter top from the underside is not especially difficult. The counter may appear to be a permanent part of the base cabinet, but chances are, like its counterpart in the kitchen, it has a separate top that is simply screwed in place from the bottom side. Once the old counter's off, a new one is attached quickly and easily.

Surfaces vary according to the look you're after. There are four basic types to choose from. A chart on pages 62 and 63 compares each in detail.

Tile

Ceramic tile makes a handsome, durable counter top. Nearly any ceramic tile will do, but all tile counters must be custom made to fit into your bath. The imported tiles *opposite, upper left* set the theme for this Mediterranean-style bath. Even the lavatory, produced by the same company that manufactured the tile, complements the overall effect. Many times, ceramic tiles are too expensive to use in great numbers. But as this bath exemplifies, a few tiles can go a long way.

Working with tile can be a challenge. Single tiles must each be stuck to the surface, with even spaces between. Using sheets of mosaic tile on a mesh or paper backing or pregrouted tile sheets are two good ways to save time and effort. Cleaning tile is easy, but grout often needs to be scrubbed. Special sealers help to prevent dirt and mildew from accumulating on the grout.

Marbles—cultured, synthetic, and natural

Cultured marble is made from real chips of natural marble embedded in plastic to look like the real thing. It's available in sheet form and in standard counter dimensions with or without a wash basin molded in. Although cultured marble is easy to clean, it must be well cared for, because once scratched, it cannot be resurfaced. Acrylic finishes on cultured marble are better than gel-coatings; they're sturdier and last longer.

Synthetic marble—like Dupont's Corian®—is also available in sheets and in ready-formed counters with integral lavatories. The material is tough; scratches, abrasions, and even burns are repaired with fine-grade sandpaper. Cut synthetic marble to desired dimensions with standard woodworking tools.

Natural marble is extraordinarily expensive and a real luxury. It stains easily, so it makes a better showpiece than it does an actual working counter top.

Plastic laminate

Long a favorite of homeowners, plastic laminate is a great material to use in the bath because it resists moisture, stains, soaps, and moderate heat. (Many people know laminate by one of its trade names—Formica®.)

For counter tops, laminate comes in large sheets, ready to be bonded to a surface of plywood or particleboard. Or it may come already bonded, with or without a backsplash. Laminate also is available formed—with a rolled edge—or it may be self-edged in a matching or contrasting color like the counter *opposite, center right*. The separate strip makes a 90-degree corner at the front edge.

Wood

Although wood counters wear well, moisture is their nemesis. For this reason, whether they're hard- or softwood, they need to be sealed with polyurethane or marine varnish.

Butcher block is a common choice. It's thicker than standard tops, so to install it, you need to modify plumbing connections. Oak or maple tongue-and-groove floorings also are handsome surfaces. The counter and backsplash *opposite, below* were made from cedar flooring, sealed with several applications of polyurethane.

(continued)

COUNTERS
(continued)

YOUR COUNTER OPTIONS

EFFECTS

TILE
Ceramic tile
Quarry tile

Ceramic tile is available in an almost endless variety of colors, shapes, designs, and textures. A matte finish is the most durable surface; it also is the least slippery when wet. Ceramic tiles are all finished with a glaze, which permanently protects them from staining. Quarry tiles, however, are not glazed and therefore are porous. You can buy sealers for both the unglazed tiles and the grout.

MARBLE
Cultured marble
Synthetic marble
Natural marble

Marble counter tops—whether natural or synthetic—provide a splendid-looking surface. Choice of colors is limited, determined by what's available locally. Even synthetic marbles are made in just a few basic colors. Marble counters have very hard surfaces; carefully choose how you want to use them.

LAMINATE
Self-edged laminate
Post-formed laminate

Laminates are available in many colors and patterns, and in some of the most convincing wood and marble look-alikes you'll ever see. Laminate finishes range in texture from high-gloss smooth to a mottled, leatherlike look. Whatever look you're after, you can find a laminate to help set the mood. Dealers usually have a few standard patterns in stock; you can order others after looking at color chips in the store.

WOOD
Butcher block
Flooring
Other kinds of wood

Natural wood makes a warm setting. Whether the decor will be sleek or rugged, there are wood surfaces available that will complement the rest of the bath. If the natural doesn't suit you, stain woods to create other tones. Also, apply boards in horizontal, vertical, or diagonal patterns to add a visually stimulating touch to the area. And wood ages well; properly sealed so it's protected from moisture, wood will last for years.

DURABILITY	USES	INSTALLATION	COSTS
Tile lasts almost indefinitely. Properly installed, it's almost as durable as stone. Grout, on the other hand, requires regular care to resist soil and mildew. A special sealer is helpful.	Luxurious, durable. Use for maximum impact. Because of the small areas to be covered, you can use this luxury material on counter tops to set a theme for the entire bath.	Often handled by the moderately skilled do-it-yourselfer. Lay tiles on a ¾-inch exterior plywood base. Spacers help set tiles evenly. Some tiles are available in sheet form; some are pregrouted.	Usually in the moderate to moderately high price range. Materials and equipment needed for installation add to the cost.
Synthetics are nonporous, hard to damage, and easy to clean with soap and water. Gloss can be restored to plastic-type synthetics. Cultured marble is easy to clean but does scratch. Natural marble is porous, prone to stains, and tough to clean.	Noisier surface. Ready-made counters are purchased with integral basins. Custom-cut sheets of material to size. Use natural marble only in powder rooms and other light-duty areas.	Most man-made marble can be handled by the do-it-yourselfer skilled enough to work with hardwood (the methods are similar). Natural marble counter tops require special structural support. Their installation is best left to experts.	Installing cultured and other synthetic marbles usually is in the moderate to moderately high price category. The price of natural marble is very high, even without considering installation charges.
Laminates resist stains and spills; they clean easily with soap and water or mild abrasive. Although the material holds up well under normal circumstances, hard blows can chip or dent the plastic. After a number of years, laminate may dull and wear thin.	Ideal for bath counters because it cleans easily and can enhance almost any decorating scheme. Resists water well so it's an excellent choice to use around lavatories, tubs, and showers.	You can order post-formed laminate tops by the running foot, with the lavatory cut out where needed; or they can be cut to your specifications. Laminating the material to particleboard or plywood is tricky. Installing finished tops is simpler.	From inexpensive to moderately expensive, depending on grade, color, texture, and pattern. Having a professional do the job adds considerably to the cost.
Rub down butcher block with oil, as needed. Flooring requires a coat of polyurethane from time to time. Wood subjected to water should be finished with marine varnish or another protective coating.	Used for vanity counter tops and other surfaces. Wood is not naturally resistant to moisture, so carefully choose the kind you want, and the ways you want to use it.	Installing laminated butcher block is a moderately difficult two-person task. Buy it by the running foot and have the supplier make needed cutouts. A counter of flooring requires a lot of assembling, cutting, fitting, and sanding.	Butcher block usually carries a high price tag. Flooring is in the medium price range, if you assemble it yourself. Buy only top-grade materials—reject any that show even the slightest warping.

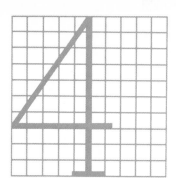

GETTING A NEW BATH ON PAPER

Adding a new bath is one of the most common projects around, yet it's also a job many homeowners shy away from doing—or even planning—themselves. Much of their reluctance has to do with the seemingly mysterious nature of a home's plumbing system. And it's true, oftentimes the nitty-gritty work should be left to an experienced plumber. However, there's no reason why you can't plan for the kind of bath you want or need. This chapter will show you how.

HOW MUCH SPACE IS AVAILABLE?

When you're thinking of a new bath, the first item on the agenda is space: Where are you going to find it? Some older houses have luxuriously large baths you can divide easily, but most baths in new homes are small, with much of the area taken up by essential fixtures. The absolute minimum space for a standard full bath—tub, toilet, and lavatory—is 5x7 feet, but, as you'll see, even within this minimum, a variety of arrangements is possible.

Money matters
Right at the start, set priorities. How much are you willing or able to spend on a new bath? Some of the job you can do on your own, but a good part of the plumbing work is likely to be beyond the skills of an average do-it-yourselfer. In all probability, you'll need a plumber's experienced hand to help you out, which means added expense. In fact, some local codes *require* that licensed plumbers do all or most of the work (see pages 78 and 79 for more information on codes and costs).

Know where the pipes are
Tight budgets and legal restrictions affect how and where you can place a new bath, but the house itself is often the biggest determining factor. Generally, plans must be adapted to existing walls and plumbing; otherwise, the entire project can become disproportionately expensive.

Plumbing is the single biggest constraint. Every dwelling has at least one plumbing "stack," which, in effect, is a system of branching pipes serving all the fixtures in your house. The system's large components—or *drainpipes*—carry wastes *away* from the house; smaller pipes—part of the *supply* system—carry hot and cold water *to* the fixtures. In addition, throughout the stack are *vent* pipes that serve each fixture; they exhaust sewer gases through an opening in the roof and provide fresh air so the drains will work smoothly.

The illustration *opposite* depicts one part of a home's plumbing stack: the multi-faceted array of pipes leading into and out of a 5x8-foot bath.

When you're planning changes, take the present system into account. Usually, it's a good idea to drain into the existing stack; it's less expensive. Adding a new stack isn't totally out of the question, but in the process, you may have to rework other plumbing in the house, along with extensive carpentry work to conceal the new pipes. Base a decision on your own needs and budget. In a house with only one bath, for example, where the demand for another is great and growing, you may want to do all you can to add another—even if the final bill is relatively high.

Templates
A template is nothing more than a pattern that's used as a guide to the arrangement of elements in a room. In the case of a bath, a template shows the configuration of fixtures within rooms of various sizes. On pages 155-157, 24 different templates are shown that can help you find a bath to fit your needs and space, whether you're remodeling or adding on.

(continued)

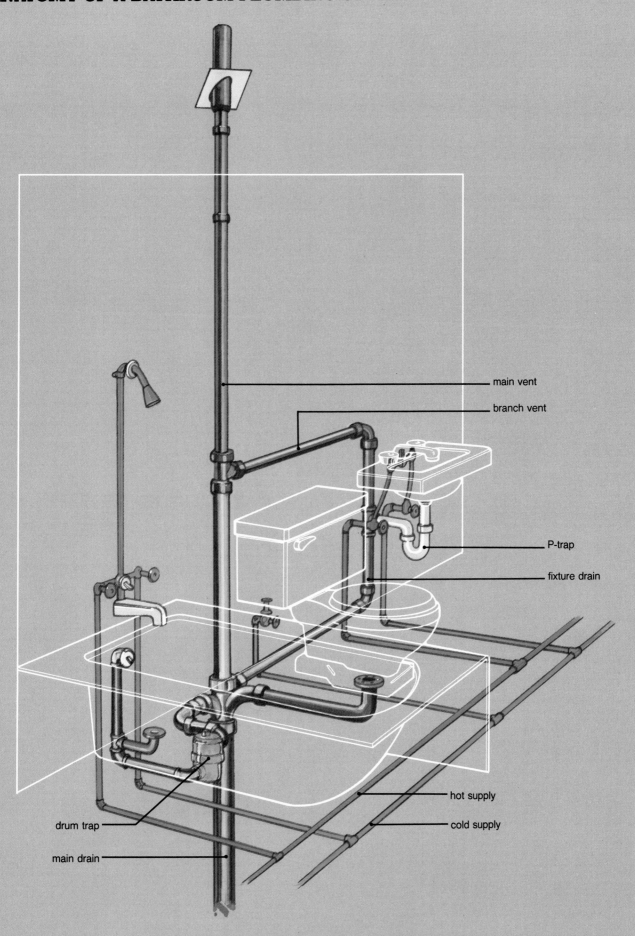

main vent

branch vent

P-trap

fixture drain

hot supply

cold supply

drum trap

main drain

HOW MUCH SPACE IS AVAILABLE?

(continued)

Templates can help you find a bath that fits, but templates alone aren't enough. A new bath affects the entire house—its livability, its appearance, the way its plumbing works. Before you look for space for a new bath, draw an accurate plan of your home as it is now—one that shows the structural features of each room *drawn to scale*. (To use our templates properly, your plan *must* be a scaled drawing.)

Don't be put off by the prospect of drawing up a precise plan. It's not as tough as it sounds.

Begin with a simple free-hand sketch of the bath and other rooms. Don't worry at this point about exact proportions or straight lines. Just draw rough shapes, indicating the locations of doors, windows, air registers, electrical fixtures, and other fixed parts of the room.

Now, using a retractable metal tape, start measuring the width of the door and window openings and distances between openings. Also note which way doors swing and the distances between other fixtures in the room. As you work, transfer each measurement to the sketch and double-check its accuracy.

Finally, convert your rough version into a finished scaled drawing using a scale of ¼ inch to the foot. The tools you'll need appear on this page: a pen or sharp pencil (an architect's pencil, like the one in the photo, is nice but not necessary), graph paper, tracing paper, masking tape, a clear plastic triangle, an architect's scale, and a T-square.

Tape a piece of tracing paper over graph paper ruled into ¼-inch squares, and draw up the rooms using the architect's scale to check your graph-paper counts and draw fractional lengths.

Begin with a freehand sketch of all the rooms, noting openings and placements of fixtures.

Always place the measuring tape over woodwork; never measure from woodwork to woodwork.

Use an architect's scale for the finished drawing. Note the exact location of each fixture.

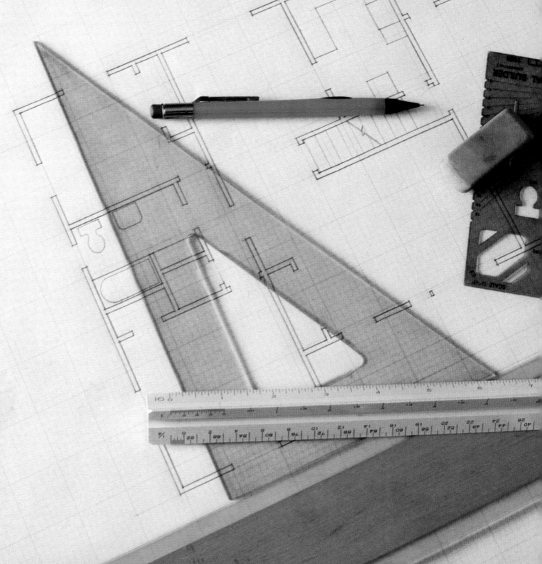

Put the "before" plan aside now and think about the way fixtures will be arranged in the new bath. Because space is at a premium, you'll have to position them carefully. The object is to provide at least minimum "clearance"—distances between fixtures or between a fixture and a wall.

If your community's building code specifies clearances, you'll have to follow its requirements. If not, let comfort be your guide, and place fixtures so you can easily move around them (and clean around them), always remembering, of course, that their layout will be influenced by the location of existing plumbing or new plumbing runs. (The measurements *at right,* including the heights of basic fixtures, are "comfortable" distances.)

Locating the toilet usually requires the most drain work, so place it first near the stack. For convenience, also try to position it next to a wall; otherwise, its drain must drop beneath the ceiling below.

Decide on a place for the tub next. The best spot is along a wall or in a corner because the floor joists ordinarily need extra support to handle the weight. Moreover, the tub should be against a wall that can be opened in case plumbing repairs are necessary.

Finally, locate the lavatory well away from the tub and toilet, making sure there's enough space around it for towel racks, cabinets, and other accessories.

The templates on pages 155-157 illustrate fixture layouts in baths of varying sizes. Simply move them around on a scaled floor plan of your house and you can see right away what might work. The following pages present a series of possibilities.

TYPICAL ELEVATION HEIGHTS

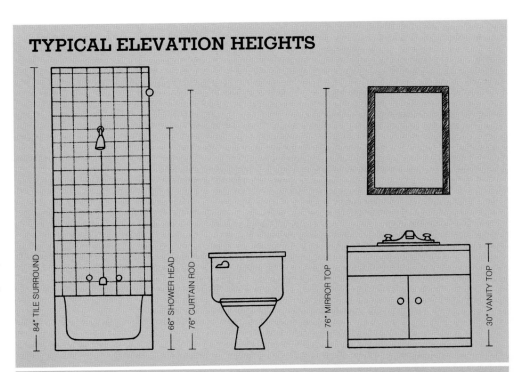

TYPICAL FIXTURE CLEARANCES

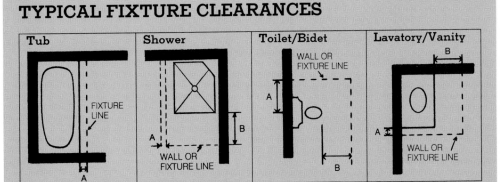

FIXTURE	A: FIXTURE CLEARANCE		B: BODY CLEARANCE	
	MINIMUM	LIBERAL	MINIMUM	LIBERAL
Tub	2″	8″		
Shower	2″	8″	18″	30″
Toilet/Bidet	12″	18″	18″	36″
Lavatory/Vanity	2″	6″	20″	30″

FOUR CASE STUDIES

SOLUTION 1: "BORROWING" CLOSET SPACE

On this page and the following three, you'll find possible ways to gain space for a new bath in four different houses. Each example has an illustration of the "before" plan done to scale, along with templates of potential choices. The solution appears as a drawing below the photograph.

The problem *at right* was to add a new bath to the upper level of a two-story house. A 5x7½-foot bath was chosen over a 5x8- or 5x7-foot one, because it required the least amount of overall remodeling.

As you can see in the drawing, the existing bedroom closet was shortened to provide access to the new bath, which takes up an old closet and the original entry to the bedroom. A new bedroom closet compensates for storage space lost in the remodeling.

BEFORE

AFTER

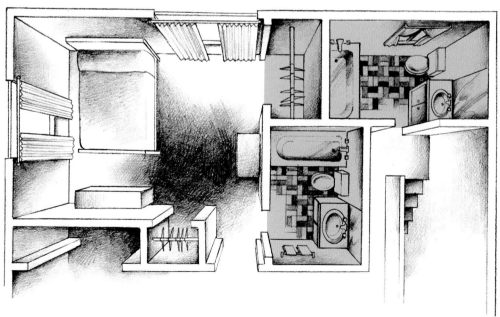

SOLUTION 2: DIVIDING AN EXISTING BATH

In this case, the problem was to use existing space in the original bath (plus some from the bedroom) to gain a new master bath.

Two layouts, both in 5x8-foot baths, looked as though they would fit in nicely. But there was an important difference between them. The first allowed the tub to remain on one exterior and two interior walls—where it was originally located—and the other required the tub to be turned.

The first choice was better: It demanded far less plumbing work to use the same fixture (and gained the same amount of space) and was, therefore, less expensive.

And even though the bedroom shrank a bit in the process, the side-by-side baths—with an extra toilet, vanity, and brand-new shower—more than made up for the smaller bedroom.

BEFORE

AFTER

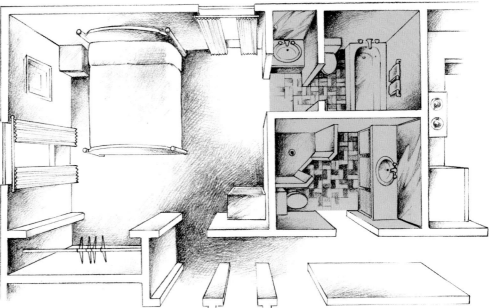

FOUR CASE STUDIES

(continued)

SOLUTION 3: SQUEEZING A HALLWAY

The goal of this project was to add a bath at the bedroom level of a split-level house. Much of the needed space was created by eliminating two linen closets and narrowing the width of the hallway from 11 to 5 feet. Of the templates shown, the three-quarter master bath fits in with the least trouble.

Nevertheless, as the drawing makes clear, the changes required quite a bit of plumbing work, even though the lines serving the tub remained in place. (The previous two solutions demonstrated that you can add a bath without moving the fixtures in the old one.) It was a lot of work to relocate the fixtures to accommodate a new design, but it did result in an extra advantage: The bedroom, unlike those in the preceding examples, didn't surrender any space to the new bath.

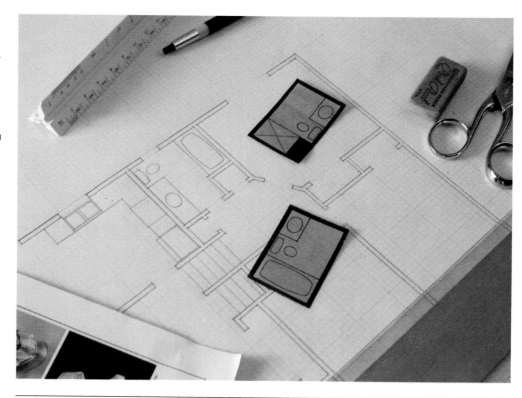

BEFORE

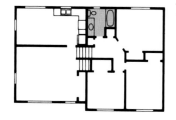

AFTER

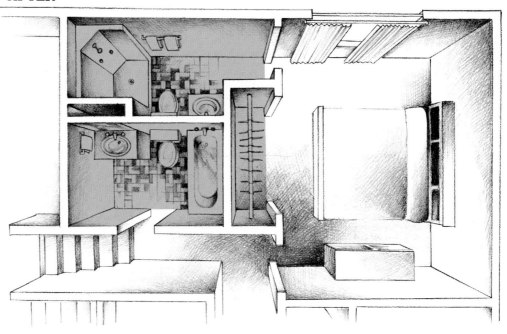

SOLUTION 4: A COMBINATION OF STRATEGIES

Here again, a bedroom gave up some space to build the new bath, which took the rest from an existing closet. The loss of space, however, was really a gain because one of the bedrooms now has a fine master bath serving it.

In this case, too, existing fixtures were moved to make the old bath roomier. Even so, if you plan correctly, the plumbing work isn't necessarily expensive or difficult.

BEFORE

AFTER

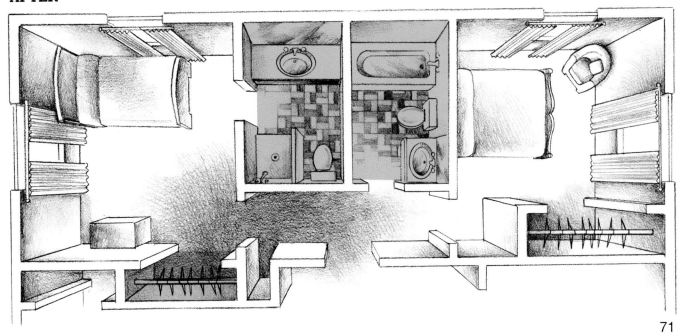

MAKING EXISTING FACILITIES MORE EFFICIENT

Sometimes, your best bath is already in place. You don't need extensive remodeling. All your existing bath may require are a few changes to make it work harder. The three solutions illustrated on these two pages will get you thinking.

• *Solution 1.* The goal here was to convert a walk-in closet into a dressing room that makes the bath more convenient and more private. Although this project demanded the most work, the changes were still relatively minor. As you can see in the "after" drawing, the lavatory was moved into the new dressing area, the tub and toilet closed off with a door, and extra closet space picked up in the spot where the vanity was originally located. The result was more privacy and new dressing facilities. In addition, the alterations make it easier to move from room to room.

• *Solution 2.* In this example, all three rooms profited from reasonably simple changes. The tub was left in place, the toilet was shifted, and a small vanity, rather than a freestanding lavatory, was installed in part of the old closet space. A large counter-top vanity was added to the lower bedroom in the drawing, which also picked up a new walk-in closet.

• *Solution 3.* This job—the easiest of the three—required no plumbing work at all. Before, occupants of the master bedroom had to go into the hallway to reach the bath. Providing direct access meant shortening an existing closet and adding a door. Now the area plays dual roles—it's not only a family bath, but a master bath, as well.

SOLUTION 1: CREATING A DRESSING ROOM

BEFORE

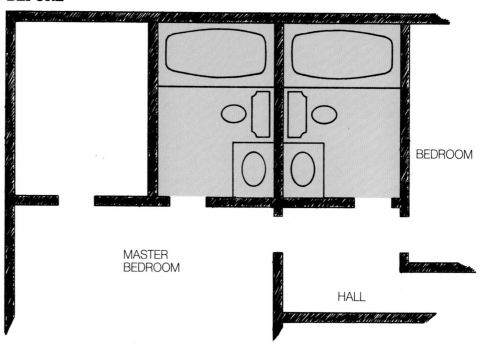

BEDROOM

MASTER
BEDROOM

HALL

AFTER

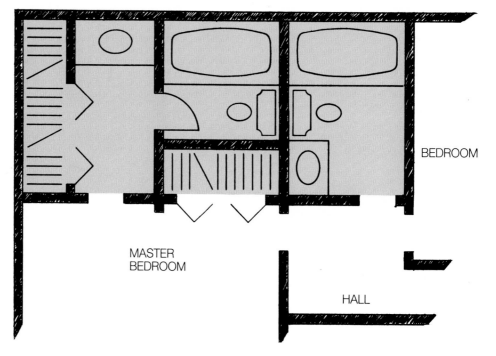

BEDROOM

MASTER
BEDROOM

HALL

SOLUTION 2:
ADDING EXTRA FUNCTION

BEFORE

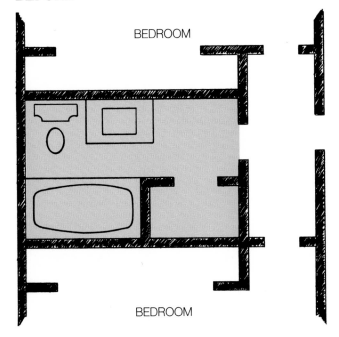

BEDROOM

BEDROOM

AFTER

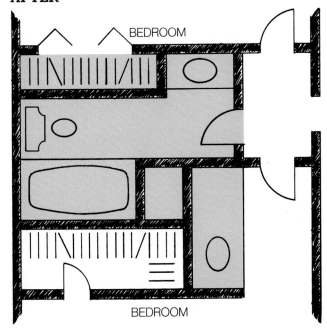

BEDROOM

BEDROOM

SOLUTION 3:
GETTING TWO FROM ONE

BEFORE

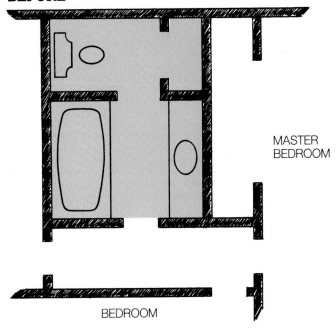

MASTER
BEDROOM

BEDROOM

AFTER

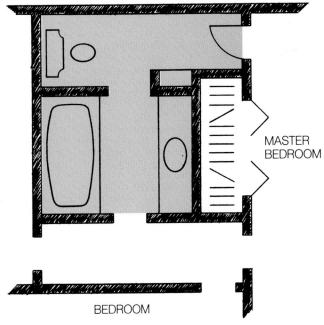

MASTER
BEDROOM

BEDROOM

73

SQUEEZING IN A HALF BATH

A half bath is often the whole answer to early-morning squabbles over who gets to wash up first. Equipped with a lavatory and toilet, a half bath can fit into very little space and serve as an efficient addition, especially if you're unable to find room for a full bath (or in case you just don't want a full bath).

Sizes vary; 4x5 and 3x7 feet are common dimensions, but a half bath—sometimes called a powder room—can be built in even smaller spaces: An area as tiny as 3x3 feet, for instance, can work effectively and comfortably. When you're searching for space to use, refer to the templates; they'll help you find the best spot.

On these two pages are six possible locations on the main level of a house for a half bath of various sizes. The overall illustration is part of the "before" floor plan.

As in every other bath project, you'll need a similarly complete plan to find out exactly how much room you have to work with. Remember, too, that the plumbing will be entirely new, perhaps relatively extensive in some cases. Don't be deterred by the prospect. Place a half bath in the most accessible, most functional spot you can find.

In addition, choose fixtures to fit the territory; in this case, those adapted for use in small spaces. With a corner-mounted lavatory and toilet, for example, you can squeeze a powder room into a spot as small as 9 square feet.

Further, storage areas should be conveniently and obviously located so guests can find bath supplies easily. Because the area is small, decor should be simple. See pages 12 and 13 for ways to perk up the appearance of a half bath.

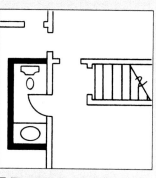

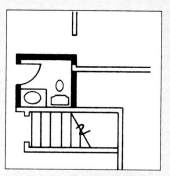

1 The location for the half bath above takes up an area 6 feet 8 inches long by 2 feet 8 inches wide. It encroaches slightly on existing garage space but provides a convenient wash-up station.

2 The solution above is a 4x5-foot bath. It utilizes room in an area near the back entry, making the bath easily accessible from the yard, minimizing traipsing through the house.

GARAGE

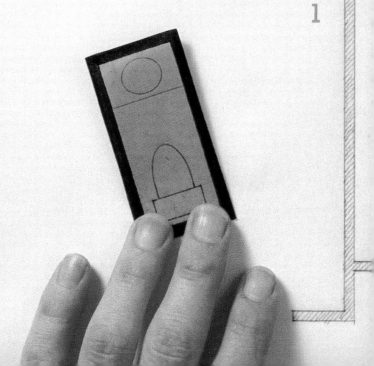

1

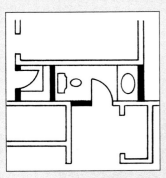

3 The 3x7-foot bath at left takes up a hallway and makes traffic flow through the house slightly more difficult. However, placing a powder room here provides an extra bonus: The plan calls for a new pantry in some of the leftover hall space.

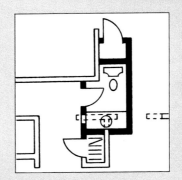

4 The 3x7-foot bath at left has an expanded leg so it doesn't block traffic flow as much as positions two and three. Although it does encroach on the dining room, additional storage space is a plus.

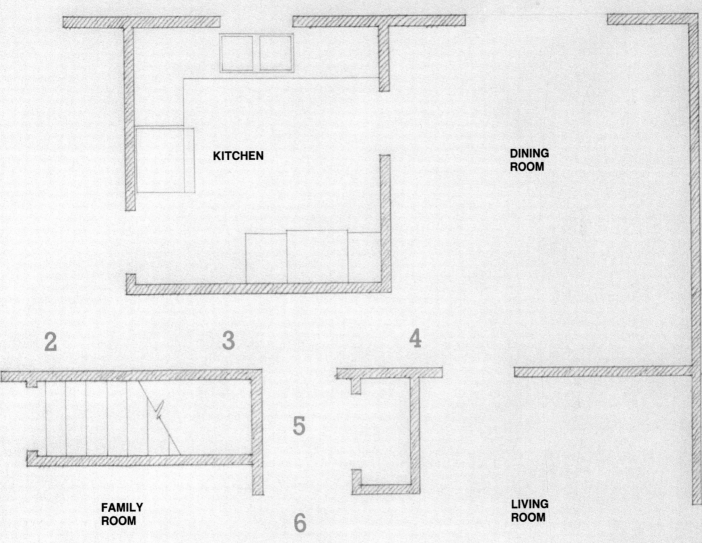

KITCHEN

DINING ROOM

2   3   4

5

FAMILY ROOM

6

LIVING ROOM

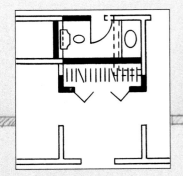

5 In another 3x7-foot area, the half bath at left uses space inside and near an entry closet next to the stairs. Even though the flow of traffic in this position is also mildly impaired, the changes do add new closet space.

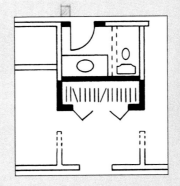

6 This half bath at left is an oddball size—4 feet deep by 7½ feet wide. Occupying approximately the same location as half bath number 5, it's a more spacious—and perhaps more glamorous—layout than the others described.

PLANNING A BATH ADDITION

Adding a bath to the exterior of a house is generally more expensive than finding room for one inside—but if you don't have space to spare, an addition may be your best bet. Before beginning, keep the following items in mind:

• Just as you would plan for a bath inside the house, make a good ''before'' drawing first, as shown *at right,* being sure to show your home's exterior features. Utilize the templates to find a size and configuration you can live with.

• Choose a spot for the addition. The job will be easier if you select a location close to existing plumbing. However, use an existing window or door opening as an access to a new bath. Dotted lines on the plan show two likely spots on the outside of this home.

• Also, think aesthetically. Pick a place where the bath *won't* be an inappropriate focal point.

• From a structural standpoint, a bath addition is handled like any other. A foundation is necessary, floor levels must be tied in, and a roof attached to the existing one. The illustration *opposite* shows how a 5x8-foot bath may shape up.

• When looking at an outside *or* an inside job, consider the relevant plumbing, electrical, and mechanical codes (see the next two pages for more information). But if you're planning an addition, also be aware of local building codes and certain aspects of real estate law that may come into play—lot line restrictions and easements, to name a couple.

• Overall, it's often wise—and certainly economical—to incorporate a bath addition into another exterior project. If you're building a deck, for instance, including a bath in the plan would take care of two needs at once.

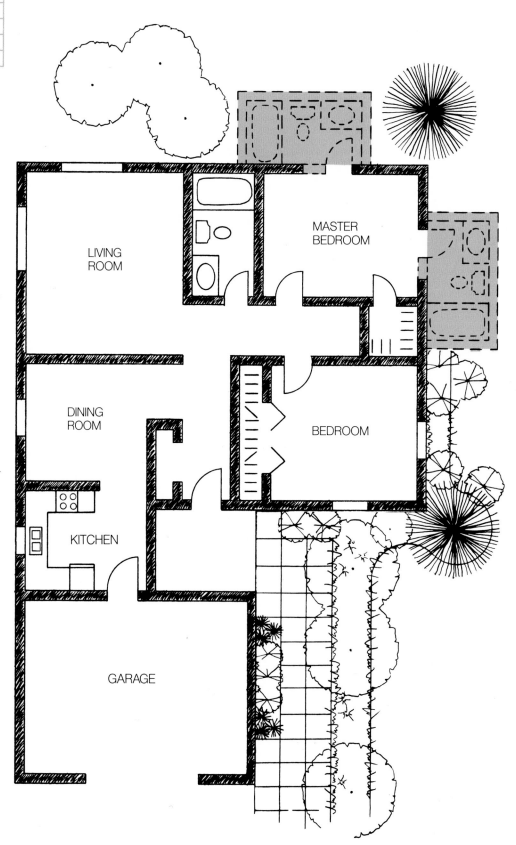

LIVING ROOM

MASTER BEDROOM

DINING ROOM

BEDROOM

KITCHEN

GARAGE

76

ANATOMY OF A BATH ADDITION

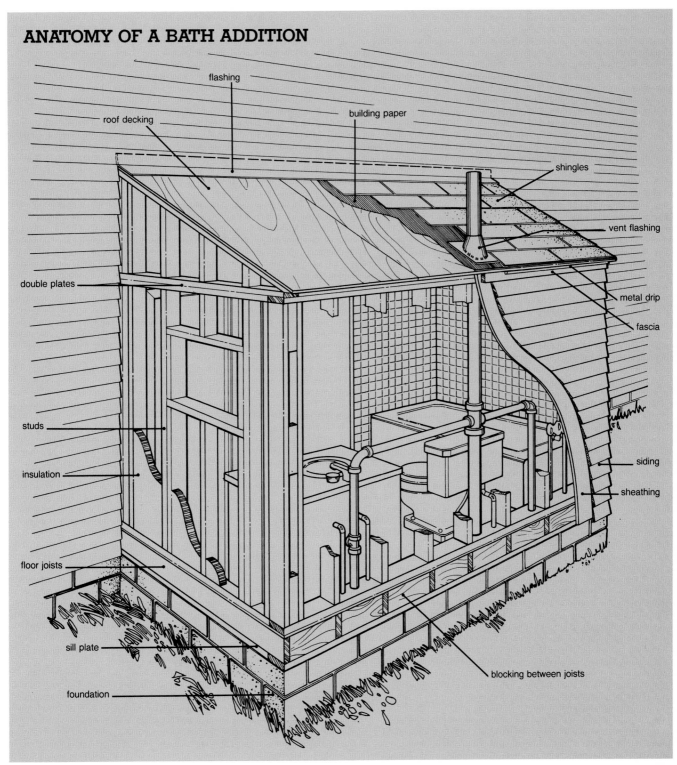

flashing

building paper

roof decking

shingles

vent flashing

double plates

metal drip

fascia

studs

insulation

siding

sheathing

floor joists

sill plate

blocking between joists

foundation

GETTING A NEW BATH ON PAPER

WHAT YOU NEED TO KNOW ABOUT CODES AND COSTS

The best-laid plans may go to waste if you're not familiar with the myriad legal restrictions that control the building of new baths and bath additions. Building, plumbing, mechanical, and electrical codes, in addition to zoning ordinances and easements, may all play a part in determining what you can and can't do. In the same way, the cost of doing certain projects is likely to influence your final decision.

Just as the structure of your house determines how realistic your plans are, so do a multitude of legal restrictions. Nearly every municipality has several codes governing construction of all kinds—including new baths and additions. Most allow homeowners to do at least part of the work themselves, as long as they receive the proper permits and arrange for inspections. Nevertheless, regulations and stipulations—and the way in which they're enforced—vary greatly from area to area. Before undertaking any project, carefully check the relevant codes in your locale.

Codes

• *Building codes* govern structural alterations. Most localities require a permit if you're going to take out a bearing wall or work on an exterior wall. A few codes also regulate less complicated tasks, like constructing or removing nonbearing partitions. In addition, nearly every community requires that ventilation—through either a window or an exhaust fan—be provided for in a new bath.

Ordinarily, before receiving a building permit, you have to submit a plan of the new bath to your community's building inspector, along with a drawing of existing structural features and how you intend to alter them. (Your "before" plan would serve adequately in most places.)

• *Plumbing codes* are notoriously varied in what they do and do not allow. Adjacent towns in the same area, for example, may have codes that differ. However, some basic points generally hold true.

Normally, homeowners can do most plumbing jobs *inside* the house, but if the work requires tie-ins to municipally owned lines, then a licensed plumber usually must take over. In some localities, a licensed plumber has to oversee specific interior alterations, as well. To find out what applies in your community—especially if you plan to do some of the project yourself—get a copy of the local code and read it thoroughly. As with structural work, you may have to draw up a plan showing both the existing system and the anticipated changes.

Plumbing codes not only determine who can do the job, but also what materials you can use and how you can use them. For instance, many communities strictly ban the installation of plastic pipe. Nearly all require that fixtures be vented individually. Moreover, the location of new drains is scrupulously regulated by most codes. If their position is more than a certain distance from an existing vent, a new vent is usually mandatory. In some cases, you may even have to make major changes in the stack. A number of codes also specify minimum clearances for a new bath's important fixtures—tub, toilet, and lavatory.

• *Mechanical* and *electrical* *codes* govern those systems in your house and may affect how you put up a new bath. Check each carefully.

Applying for permits may take time, so investigate them well before you want the work to begin. Applications are usually available at municipal offices, local libraries, and building departments. Determine, too, what plans are necessary and how many copies you'll need to prepare for each permit.

Ordinances and easements

Zoning ordinances may influence your work if you plan to construct a bath addition. Like plumbing codes, local regulations vary—some are extremely restrictive; others, lenient. Most, however, specify the distance your house must be from the side, front, and rear boundaries of your property. If your planned addition conflicts with the ordinance, you may have to apply for a "variance" with the local zoning commission.

While you're planning, read the deed to your property to make sure easements won't prevent your putting up a bath exactly where you want to. Those that often come into play allow a utility company to lay cables or water mains across part of your property.

Costs

The final bill for a new bath or addition obviously depends on the extent of the changes and the amount of work you do on your own. However, keep the following points in mind:

• To hold down costs, do as much of the planning as possible. Though an addition may require professional advice, you should be able to do much of the preliminary work for a new bath inside the house. When planning, keep structural changes to a minimum.

• Plumbing work done by a professional is expensive—well over $30 an hour in many places. Nevertheless, in most cases, you'll need the help of a licensed plumber.

• Building a bath addition means, inevitably, higher property taxes. You can often estimate the increase in advance by calling the assessor's office, describing the work you're doing, and noting the estimated cost of the addition. Some communities will routinely issue a higher tax bill if you use certain building materials.

PRICING PLUMBING: THREE EXAMPLES

PROJECT	CODE CONSIDERATIONS	RELATIVE COST
RELOCATING A LAVATORY OR TUB	Nearly all plumbing codes require that lavatories and tubs be "wasted" and "vented" properly, which means that drainpipes can be no more than a certain distance from an existing vent. If they are, you must install a new vent. In addition, most codes stipulate that overflow be provided for in a lavatory, so the faucet is never submerged in dirty water. Also, some codes specify minimum clearances between fixtures and between fixtures and walls.	With a plumber doing the work at approximately $30 an hour, relocating a lavatory or tub in a 5x7-foot bath generally costs between $200 and $250 for each fixture.
RELOCATING A TOILET	Codes require that toilets be wasted and vented adequately. Some codes also define a minimum room size in which a toilet can be located. Minimum clearances may be specified, as well.	The cost of relocating a toilet in a 5x7-foot bath runs between $200 and $250, assuming a plumber does the job at about $30 an hour.
INSTALLING A NEW STACK	Most codes govern the kinds of materials to be used in the stack. They also stipulate that it must extend full size, uninterrupted to "blue sky," meaning it must come to a certain specified distance above the roof line. Codes also regulate the distance between the stack's point of exit and other openings in the roof or sidewall. Nearly all codes require that the stack vent increase in size at the roof line so it can't be closed by frost. In addition, codes define the proper position of offsets and vents within the stack.	A plumber working at around $30 an hour will usually install a new stack of pipes in a single-story house for about $500; in a two-story house, the cost will be about $100 more.

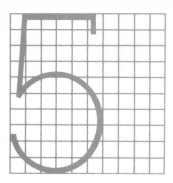

SELECTING BATHROOM COMPONENTS

Baths are busy places. The things you put in them should not only look good, but—more importantly— they should work without fail day after day after day. This chapter is a basic guide to choosing the right components—from big-ticket essentials like lavatories, toilets, and tubs, to smaller accessories that make a bath an easier place to live in. Match the advice to your bath, don't skimp on quality, and you'll have a room that won't let you down.

LAVATORIES

When you're shopping for lavatories, you'll find many shapes and sizes—from sleek, sculptural pedestal units to designs with special features for shampooing. You'll discover contemporary hexagons and triangles, along with the more traditional squares, rectangles, circles, and ovals. Lavatories are available in a variety of materials, too.

• *Porcelainized cast iron* is extraordinarily durable, but heavy, which means it needs a sturdy support system.

• *Enameled steel* doesn't wear as well but is especially good when you're remodeling because it's light enough to move into place easily.

• *Stainless steel* is light, durable, and unaffected by household chemicals, but the steel tends to collect spots from hard water and soap residue.

• *Vitreous china* is easy to clean and has a lustrous surface, but can crack or chip when struck with a heavy object.

• *Fiber-glass reinforced plastic* can be molded into novel shapes, but it doesn't hold a shine as well as other surfaces.

• *Marbleized china* has all the sterling qualities of the best natural china.

• *Simulated* or *cultured marble* is handsome, but abrasive cleaners may spoil the finish.

Mounting systems
Just as lavatories vary in shapes, sizes, and materials, they are mounted in a number of ways; basically they hang from the wall, stand on their own pedestals, or rest in vanity cabinets.

• *Self-rimming,* or *surface-mounted,* lavatories feature a ridge around the bowl that fits over the counter top to form a tight seal. The ridge also prevents water from splashing onto the counter.

• A *flush-mounted* lavatory is recessed into the counter top with a tight-fitting metal rim around the bowl. The rim comes in different finishes to match the faucet. With this model, water frequently escapes onto the counter, making the rim joint hard to clean.

• A *recessed* lavatory fits under the counter top (which has a cutout in the surface) and also is difficult to clean around the edge.

• *One-piece integral* lavatories are molded with no joint or separation between the bowl and counter top.

How big is big enough?
Generally, choose the largest lavatory you can fit into your bath. It's more comfortable to use and minimizes splashing onto the floor. You'll find bowls ranging in size from a compact 12x31 inches to an expansive 22x44 inches.

Counter tops are usually 31 to 34 inches high, although 36-inch counters are more comfortable for taller individuals. Lower versions are also available for children.

If you install two lavatories in the same counter, allow a minimum of 12 inches between them and 8 inches at each end of the counter.

If your bath is small, you may want to avoid large vanities (even though the storage space is useful). Instead, choose a pedestal lavatory or one that hangs on the wall; each takes up less space.

TOILETS AND BIDETS

In recent years, toilets have undergone a change of face. The modern versions—in a wide array of designs and styles—are sleeker and quieter, and use water more efficiently. And as appearances change, so do customs: Bidets, which are popular in Europe, also have been slowly easing their way into American baths.

Today's toilets come in so many different styles, shapes, and colors, it's easy to be misled by all the flashiness. Don't dive right into the market and select a toilet at first sight. Before making your choice, keep in mind a few basic facts.

What to look for

Take a good look at the space available in your bath. How much room is there between the wall and the center of the floor flange? Usually, the distance is 12 inches, but in some baths, it's only 10 inches. Whatever the measurement, your new toilet has to match precisely.

Conservation is another characteristic to look for. Each flush represents a lot of water down the drain—5 to 7 gallons in most toilets. Nevertheless, you can buy models that use as few as 3½ gallons per flush. In addition, certain toilets are designed to work well even when the water pressure is low, a common problem in many areas.

Moreover, contemporary toilets don't have to sound off every time you use them. Ask about features in the flushing mechanism designed to control noise. Similarly, the valve regulating the flow from the tank should operate smoothly and quietly to maintain a constant level of water in the bowl.

Most manufacturers know that cleaning a toilet is not likely to be your favorite pastime. Look for styles with accessible bases, which you can scrub around easily. Some companies even produce a wall-mounted model, suspended a few inches above the floor; cleaning is no more enjoyable, but at least it takes less time.

Finally, nearly all toilets are made of vitreous china, which is markedly durable but, like most other hard surfaces, may chip if you drop a heavy object on it.

What's the difference?

Although the material is generally the same, the choice of styles and colors is definitely not. Toilets are a varied lot.

• *Integral units.* Some toilets feature tank and bowl combined into one low-to-the-floor piece. Ordinarily, their flushing sound is quieter than standard styles with the water tank above the bowl.

• *Bowl shapes.* Round bowls are most common, but some toilets have elongated bowls that are 2 inches longer, front to back, than their conventional cousins. Besides being easier to sit on, they're easier to clean.

• *Wall-hung toilets.* If you don't want to cut through concrete when you're installing a toilet, select one with waste outlets in the wall instead of the floor.

• *The space-saver.* Not much room in your bath? A triangular toilet fits neatly into a 2x2-foot corner.

• *Special features.* Some toilet tanks are insulated to stop water from condensing on the surface. Another model has an internal ventilation system designed to prevent odors. Still other toilets—those you install in the basement, for example—are built to flush upward.

• *For the disabled.* Toilet seats with arms projecting from them help in standing up and sitting down. One model is 18 inches high, compared to the normal 14 inches; the extra height makes it easier to use. For more about fitting out a bath for a disabled person, see pages 150 and 151.

• *Interior design.* Toilets not only look different on the outside, they also work differently on the inside. The most common design, known as a *reverse trap,* flushes through an outlet in the back. Reverse-trap toilets are efficient and relatively quiet.

Siphon-jet toilets improve on the reverse-trap design. This one also flushes through the back, but has a larger outlet that drains faster and more efficiently. Siphon-jet toilets are nearly silent, and cost considerably more than reverse-trap types.

A third variety of flushing action—the *washdown* toilet—is all but obsolete. It drains through the front of the bowl, usually with a loud glugging sound, and is the least efficient of all. You'll probably not find a washdown toilet at most plumbing suppliers; they're prohibited by codes in many areas. If yours is an older home with wash-down toilets, definitely consider replacing them with reverse-trap or siphon-jet types.

Bidets

When the health-and-fitness boom hit this country with a bang, some manufacturers began to offer bidets again (in designs and colors to match their toilets). The height of a chair seat, most take up a 3x3-foot space next to the wall near the toilet and require hot and cold water, in addition to a drain pipe. To use a bidet, simply sit astride it, facing the faucets. A gentle spray allows you to clean genital and posterior areas.

To save space, you can also buy combination toilet/bidet units that incorporate both functions in a single fixture—or convert an ordinary toilet with a special seat.

TUBS AND SHOWERS

Tubs and showers have become more than just conveniently utilitarian places to clean up, cool down, or clear out the cobwebs after a good night's sleep. The emphasis today is on the bath or shower as a pleasurable, relaxing experience. As a result, your choice of styles, sizes, materials, and colors is staggeringly diverse. Here's what to know before you buy.

Size up your bath first. Except for a thorough-going remodeling, you probably won't take the time—or spend the money—to relocate plumbing and drain lines. So the new tub has to fit the old space.

Consider, too, how you're going to remove the used tub and bring in the new. Some tubs simply won't make it through standard doorways; you may have to break apart the existing fixture or remove part of a wall (see pages 98 and 99 for more information). Getting a new unit in can be easier if you buy a shower-tub kit that comes pre-formed in two or three sections to fit easily through most doors.

Material differences

Most tubs are built from one of three common materials.

• *Fiber-glass reinforced plastic* is highly malleable and can be molded into many shapes. Most tubs made from it weigh between 60 and 70 pounds, are sturdily reinforced, and are warmer to the touch than others. Although this material doesn't chip easily, if at all, abrasive cleaners will damage the surface. In addition, install-ing the tub is sometimes a dif-ficult job—all edges and stress points must be fully supported.

• *Molded cast iron* (with a por-celain enamel surface) makes an extraordinarily durable tub. It also makes an extraordinarily heavy tub—from 350 to 500 pounds. Like fiber glass, cast iron keeps water warm for a long time.

• *Formed steel* tubs (also with a porcelain enamel surface) are less expensive than cast iron and not nearly so heavy. They usually weigh between 120 and 125 pounds. Also, water cools down more quickly in a formed steel tub than in

one made from fiber-glass reinforced plastic or cast iron, and steel tubs are prone to chipping and denting.

Shapes galore

You'll see tubs in every shape imaginable. A typical tub is 5 feet long, but you also can find them as short as 4½ feet and as long as 6 feet.

Other tubs are delightfully different: square, oblong, oval, or round. Even a low, square receptor tub is available to double as the base for a shower.

Some tubs are self-rimming, meant to be installed in a built-in platform. A number of tubs are designed to fit into a recess or alcove without a special platform.

Wonder showers

Ordinary shower stalls range in size from a compact 32 inches square, up to 48 inches. Gen-erally, a comfortable minimum is 36 inches.

You can buy stalls with a steam unit included. Most have a built-in bench; sliding tem-pered-glass doors keep the steam inside. (More about steam units on page 116.)

Also available are self-contained chambers that provide simulated sun, wind, and rain—all at the flick of a switch.

Other features

Safety first—always—in a tub or shower. Look for nonslip bottoms and built-in grab bars. Check, too, for back supports, headrests, and armrests.

Finally, be aware of small but attractive special features. For example, you can buy a tub with the drain opposite the faucets, not directly below them. Cleaning one of these is a simpler chore.

SELECTING BATHROOM COMPONENTS

When you're choosing fittings, you want faucets and shower heads that not only fit into the overall design of the bath, but are eye-catching in their own right as well. At the same time, you also want fittings that won't give you fits: They must *work* consistently well, or all their good looks will only add up to a set of expensive headaches.

FAUCETS AND SHOWER HEADS

Many bathtubs and lavatories are sold without fittings so you can select exactly the ones you want. You'll find a stunning variety of materials and styles, ranging from basic chrome (the best is double-plated) to glitzy golden faucets with jewel-studded handles. In between, you'll find alternatives: china, brass, and plastic, to name a few.

Faucet fare
Viewed from the outside, there are two kinds of faucets—those with two handles and those with one. The former are more traditional; the latter more modern and able to do double-duty by mixing hot and cold water while simultaneously controlling the flow.

Both faucets are constructed in one of two ways. A *center set* is installed as a single piece in the middle of the lavatory or tub. With a *spread set,* individual parts of the fitting go into separate holes. In either case, be sure the fittings match the spacing of the holes in your lavatory or tub.

Inside, regardless of the external design, all faucets either have washers (compression) or they don't (noncompression). To compare the quality of the two, check a number of manufacturers' warranties.

The standard compression valve, which has been on the market for years, operates with a threaded stem and occasionally needs a new washer. It always has separate controls for hot and cold water.

Updated two-handle faucets use diaphragms or cartridges instead of threads. The result is less wear from friction. (For exploded views of all three types, see page 148.)

Three single-lever faucets are popular in bathrooms.

The *rotating-ball* faucet is most common. To change the water's volume and temperature, move the lever up and down, right and left, or two directions at the same time.

The *disk* faucet mixes hot and cold water with a pair of disks that raise, lower, and rotate inside the faucet body.

The *sleeve-cartridge* faucet works with a single lever and a single cam that controls the flow. If the faucet needs repair, replace the whole cartridge.

(More about single-lever faucets on page 149.)

The price you pay
Aside from the decorative touches on the outside, the price of faucets is usually determined by the quantity and quality of the brass inside. An assembly made entirely of brass resists corrosion the best but is relatively expensive. Don't buy an inexpensive faucet from an unknown manufacturer. Repairs may be frequent, and parts difficult—or impossible—to find.

You also can choose among a wide array of special features—from spray attachments to swing spouts. Each raises the price a little more.

Heads up
Many shower fittings are combined with faucets in the tub; a transfer valve diverts water from one fitting to the other. Moreover, some shower heads allow you to control the volume, set up a pulsating flow, and even preset temperatures to avoid the shock of unexpectedly hot or cold water. Water-saving shower heads can be shut off while you soap. Finally, hand-held showers can serve as adjustable heads with a fitting that slides up and down a rod to precisely the height you want.

SELECTING BATHROOM COMPONENTS

ANTIQUE FIXTURES

Remodeling doesn't necessarily mean you must use the latest styles and materials. Re-creating a vintage bath is an elegant way to transform a nondescript room into a nostalgic delight. To make the change, use either original fixtures or modern versions of them. Here's how to select wisely.

Compared to their contemporary counterparts, nineteenth-century baths were distinctively roomy. Tubs were larger, ceilings were higher, and windows were bigger. But old baths were also likely to be poorly heated and plagued by a constant shortage of hot water.

Getting a fix on fixtures
Fortunately, today's homes are more efficient, and you can concentrate on bringing back the past by finding the right fixtures.

If you're looking for original items, the search may be tough. One place to check is a local salvage yard. Even better, try combing the neighborhood for old houses that are about to be demolished. They may contain just what you're looking for.

When you do find the genuine article, examine its surface. Around the turn of the century, for example, cast-iron enameled tubs were popular. However, the enamel tended to wear off quickly. By 1910, most tubs had a more durable porcelain enamel surface. With either model, if a fixture is badly worn, it can be restored by a firm that specializes in resurfacing porcelain.

Small chips are not much trouble either. They're probably inconspicuous and may be on a side that doesn't show.

Cast-iron sinks, like the pedestal version *above,* also can be resurfaced. China sinks cannot. If you find one that's badly stained, you may be able to clean it up with the technique explained on page 145. You can't do much about hairline cracks and crazing, though, and might decide that these add to the fixture's antique charm.

Working parts, such as drain assemblies and faucets, may need replating, but first check with a plumber to make sure internal parts aren't badly worn. You may be better off investing in modern-day reproductions. Bear in mind that simple hardware styles may be more authentic than overly ornate pieces, which weren't the fashion late in the nineteenth century.

Old-fashioned toilets can be updated with modern-day flush mechanisms: Several manufacturers even offer brand-new parts for pull-chain toilets—including oak flush tanks. But, do beware of the obsolete washdown bowls described on page 83.

SELECTING BATHROOM COMPONENTS

TOWEL BARS AND OTHER HARDWARE

Don't back off after selecting a lavatory, tub, and toilet. Your next job is to add those small items that make a bath work as well as it should: towel bars, grab bars, soap dishes, toilet-paper dispensers, toothbrush holders, even a hook for your bathrobe. Give them special places, conveniently and safely located. And don't skimp on quality! Each accessory should look right at home with all those carefully chosen fixtures.

SHOWER ENCLOSURES

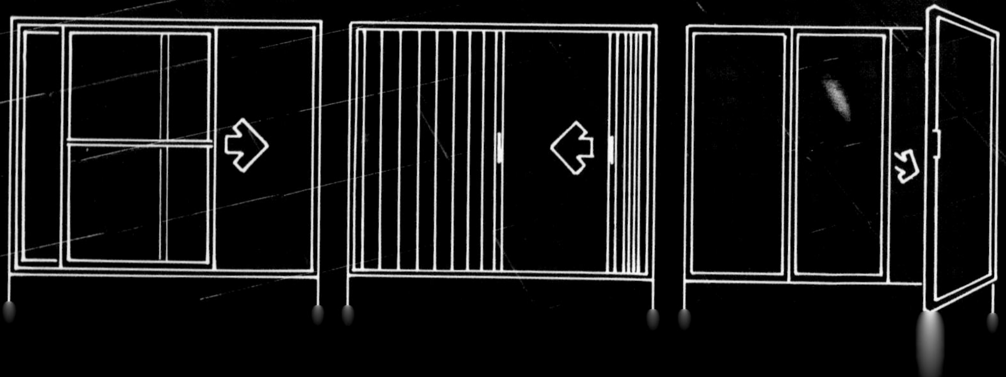

From sleek contemporary to mellow antique, no matter what style you choose for bathroom components, you'll find hardware that can follow through.

Towel and grab bars

Towel bars are made of many favorite things: polished chrome, brushed chrome, antiqued brass, 24-carat gold, clear and opaque plastic, wood, brass, aluminum, porcelain, ceramic, and glass. Use the latter with care, of course, and perhaps not at all if there are children in the family.

Metal bars should be double-plated to make them more durable. Gold plating is soft (let alone expensive) and wears down quickly in well-traveled baths. Reserve it for the guest powder room or the master bedroom suite.

Ideally, each person using the bath should have at least 36 inches of towel bar, to accommodate a hand and a bath towel. Hung separately, hand towels fit nicely on bars 18 inches long; bath towels need ones at least 24 inches in length. Install the bars 36 to 42 inches from the floor.

Screw the bars and other accessories firmly to the wall, even if you have to drill holes in the tile. Hollow wall anchors (either expanding or wing) work well in drywall. In any event, don't rely only on adhesives; they're not powerful enough to hold things in place.

Towel rings take up less space than bars and also fit neatly into out-of-the-way corners. But towels draped over them won't dry as quickly.

Grab bars are either straight or angular. Install the straight version in a tub; the L-shaped, angular variety is effective in a combination bath and shower.

Regardless of the shape they're in, grab bars must be strong. Most are made of solid brass tubing, welded stainless steel, or brazed solid brass. Mount them with a secure anchoring device that ensures the rail will stay put.

Shower doors

With shower enclosures, think safety first, then convenience. For safety, any enclosure should be made of tempered glass, acrylic, or other non-breakable material. The most popular *bypass* units consist of two doors, one or both of which may slide open. *Accordion* doors are easy to install but not quite as durable as solid doors and more difficult to clean. *Swinging* doors make sense only in baths big enough to accommodate the arcs of their swings.

Custom touches

Step into most hardware or bath specialty stores, and you'll see a bonanza of other accessories for the bath in a wide range of styles. Some are optional, such as the telescoping towel rod and retractable laundry line shown *at near left*, but two pieces you'll definitely need are soap dishes and toilet-paper dispensers; they can be surface-mounted or recessed into the wall.

The same goes for medicine cabinets. Recessed versions are sized to fit between wall studs; others surface-mount, which you may need to do in a bath with pipes in the wall behind the lavatory. Many medicine cabinets come with integral lighting fixtures, and some have a hinged, triple mirror that swings out for a three-way view.

EXHAUST FANS, LIGHTING FIXTURES, AND HEATERS

The best-equipped bath in the world would be a sorry place indeed if lighting and ventilation were inadequate. So much activity takes place in this room—often so quickly—that being able to see clearly is more than a convenience—it's a necessity. Similarly, exhaust fans, often required by local building codes, help to keep the air clear and fresh. In some baths, too, auxiliary heaters are welcome additions.

Shower, bath. Shower, bath. Dry. Wet. Damp. More than any room in your house, the bath is a spot where the environment changes rapidly each day. An adequate ventilation system helps you to even out those changes—preventing walls and ceilings from peeling, mirrors from fogging, and condensation from collecting on tile surfaces.

Fans

Generally, local building codes require ventilation fans in baths without windows. But even if your bath *does* have windows, installing a fan is a good idea, especially if you live in a humid climate or one where cold weather precludes opening windows.

How to pick? Fans are sized by numerical designations according to their ability to move air in a minute's time. Called cubic-foot-per-minute (CFM) ratings, the numbers allow you to choose a unit built to handle the space in your bath.

A quick, accurate way to determine the right rating is to multiply the bath's square footage by 1.07. A 5x9-foot room, for instance, requires at least a 48-CFM fan. And because units are sized in increments of 10, a 50-CFM model would be your choice.

Fans also differ in the amount of noise they make. On the rating plate, you'll find a number called a *sone rating,* which measures sound produced. The lower the rating, the quieter the fan. A 4-sone model, for example, makes only half as much noise as one rated at 8 sones.

Where to put it? Mount ventilation fans in the ceiling or wall, ideally near the tub or

shower. If you like, wire the fan to your light switch, so both go on simultaneously. Or install a separate switch. Before beginning, however, check the building codes again. In some places, windowless baths must have fans that begin working when the lights go on.

If possible, install the fan so it discharges moisture-laden air to the outside. Duct into a well-ventilated attic or crawl space, using specially built channels that are part of the unit.

In addition, for the fan to work properly, you have to provide a passage for air coming into the bath from other parts of the house. Louvered panels in the door or a door that's cut off slightly at the bottom will do the job well.

Most bathroom fans have only one speed, although you can find models with more. And some fans are fancier than others: They come equipped with heat lamps or lights, or both.

Light, more light

Good lighting in a bath is critical, and usually, to cover the territory, you need two kinds—general and task. For either type, if you choose fluorescent lighting, pick out deluxe warm-white tubes; they're more flattering to skin tones. If you choose incandescent lighting, select warm-white bulbs. In either case, remember that a bath decorated in dark colors will need more wattage because dark tones absorb more light. In contrast, you may have to cut back a little if the wall covering is bright and shiny.

For general lighting, most baths need about 30 lumens of light—approximately 150

watts for a 5x8-foot area or 4 watts of incandescent light per square foot (2 per square foot if you're using fluorescent lighting fixtures).

Many different kinds of fixtures provide even, general lighting. Track lights, for example, are adjustable to illuminate dark spots in the room. Another option is to make the entire ceiling a light fixture by using luminous panels. Needless to say, use moistureproof fixtures over a tub or in a shower.

Task lighting is also important, particularly if the bath has separate compartments. For instance, light around the mirror should be diffuse, without glare, and pointed toward the person, not at the mirror. In any event, don't rely solely on overhead lighting to take care of this spot—it causes false shadows.

Depending on your needs you may also want to add a small night-light, a sunlamp, an infrared heat lamp, or an ozone lamp to freshen the air.

Heaters

Though not so important as good lighting and sound ventilation, heaters are a comfortable addition to many baths—especially if you don't want to shiver the instant you step out of the shower.

To remedy the problem, install a supplementary heater in the wall or ceiling. Be sure to place a wall heater where it won't burn towels or curtains or singe the backside of an unwary bather.

Use either built-in electric or gas heaters. An electric model must be properly grounded. Gas heaters must be vented. Some varieties have timing devices, and some are combined with lighting or venting equipment. Under most circumstances, stay away from portable heaters.

WATER SOFTENERS, PURIFIERS, AND FILTERS

Water, water everywhere, and we never stop to think where it all comes from or how it arrives so fresh and pure. As a matter of fact, in many parts of the country, people need to *work* on their water before they can use it. In their homes, special softeners tame hard water, and filters remove unwanted minerals and sediment. As a result, the treated water is more serviceable in cooking, cleaning, bathing, and operating appliances or mechanical equipment.

People lucky enough to live where the water is naturally soft, tasteless, clean, and odorless don't know how soft they have it. Hard water is the most common problem—and calcium and magnesium are the primary culprits. They're picked up—along with other substances—as rain falls through the atmosphere to the ground. While the water seeps into the soil, additional impurities tag along, so that by the time it reaches a reservoir, the water may also include traces of iron, calcium bicarbonate, sulfur, and manganese, in addition to carbon dioxide, chlorides, sulfates, nitrates, and ammonia.

As if these weren't enough, water also can acquire impurities from the supply system itself. Corroded particles of lead, zinc, copper, and iron from pipes are common contaminants.

Of course, municipal purifying plants remove most of the junk before it reaches your home. Even so, the water—though safe—may still taste bad and cause other difficulties. And if your home's water comes from a well, it may be downright undrinkable.

Hard problems

Hard water often irritates the skin. More commonly, many people have stood in a shower and faced one of the most annoying problems associated with hard water: soap that refuses to lather. In fact, the hardness of water is measured by the quantity of a standard soap solution necessary to produce a certain amount of lather.

To test your water for hardness, draw off a pint into a bottle you can cap, add 10 drops of detergent, and shake well. If the solution foams readily, your water is relatively soft. If you get a curdlike film instead of foam, consider investing in a water softener.

The soft life
Softened water may not be a miracle cure for every household ailment, but it definitely makes life easier.
• Softened water means you need less soap for bathing or showering because it lathers readily, rinses off quickly, and doesn't create a sticky curd. Shampooing is simpler for the same reasons.
• Because it works more efficiently, softened water permits you to use less soap or detergent in the laundry.
• Hard water tends to leave a greasy film behind, making dishwashing a frustrating battle. In contrast, any object cleaned with soft water is *really* cleaned and not left with a hard-water residue clinging to it.
• Plumbing systems work more effectively because the water heater, pipes, shower heads, and faucets don't collect a corrosive scale caused by hard water. (A ⅛-inch buildup in the heater can boost the cost of hot water by nearly 20 percent.)

Conditioned response
Water conditioners (or softeners) bring the above benefits into your home. They come in two basic kinds. One is a compact cabinet containing the entire unit. The second, which has a larger capacity, consists of two tanks, including an extra-large container for storing salt.

Typically, the cabinet measures 2 feet long, 2 feet wide, and 4 feet high. In the larger version, one tank usually measures 12 inches in diameter and 4 feet high; the other, approximately 20 inches in diameter and 3 feet high. Both units are small enough to fit unobtrusively in a laundry or utility room. If you live in a warm climate, you can even put them outside, with or without a protective shed.

How does a water conditioner work? Simply. Each unit has a column of resin which captures the impurities that make water hard. The resin is then bathed in a salt solution, which removes the impurities and flushes them through a drain. Meanwhile, the resin is rinsed of the salt and is ready to begin another cycle. (In the more sizable conditioners, one tank contains resin; the other, salt.)

No matter how much water you use, the process is automatic. The resin lasts for years, although you have to replace the salt from time to time. In addition, the salt tank must be cleaned out once every two years.

If for some reason you *want* to use hard water (when sprinkling the lawn, for instance), you can buy a special valve that allows water to bypass the conditioner temporarily.

Filters
Whereas softeners don't actually *clean* the water as such, filtration systems thoroughly remove particulate impurities. Water from private wells, which may have specific particulates suspended in it, is often filtered before use. You may want to employ a filtration system even if you're not drinking well water—to get

the purest liquid you can. (If you use both a softener *and* a filter, filter first and soften second.)

Analysis of a water sample (see below) will determine the kind of system you need. One type uses charcoal to remove bad tastes and odors. Another removes iron or hydrogen sulfide. Still another kind works to lower the acidity of water, thereby lessening its corrosive power.

Like water conditioners, filters also vary in size and scope. Full-line filtration systems treat all the water in the house; smaller units handle specific jobs, usually filtering water in the kitchen for cooking and drinking. Full-line systems are about 12 inches in diameter and up to 5 feet high. The more restricted filters are only 4 inches in diameter and 12 to 14 inches high.

Taking a sample
If ground water is your source of supply, a careful analysis by a county agency or private laboratory is often a good idea. Here's how to draw a sample:

Choose an indoor, leak-free faucet; remove its aerator or strainer. Next, sterilize the inside of the spout with a propane torch; when you're done, don't touch the spout.

Now run the water at full flow for five minutes. Reduce to the diameter of a pencil and run for another minute.

Fill a sterile bottle three-quarters of the way up. Don't touch the inside of the bottle or cap. Close immediately, and take it to the laboratory or public office, or store according to their instructions.

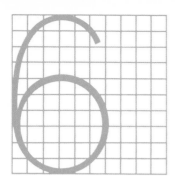

HOW TO ADD OR REMODEL A BATH

Remodeling an old bath or adding a new one is among the most popular home improvement projects in America. As a total, start-to-finish project, taking apart a bath and putting it back together again are beyond most amateurs' skills. But you may be able to do more than you think. What's more, if you understand the basics common to every bathroom project, you'll be better able to deal with a contractor and better equipped to plan the right bath for your family.

GETTING STARTED

Just as a washed-up bath is a daily irritation, a new or remodeled bath brings pleasure and efficiency for years—and also may add substantially to the value of your house.

The dreary bath *below* no longer met the needs of a family of four. Part of a 50-year-old house, it was too cramped, with no shower and an ancient tub that was hard to clean. To make matters worse, the vanity shown in the photograph was more trouble than it was worth—it blocked the door.

The owners solved their problem by knocking out a wall and incorporating the adjacent linen closet and part of a clothes closet. They then shifted the positions of the toilet and lavatory, providing more privacy and more space. Finally, new fixtures, including a tub, completed the dramatic metamorphosis *at right* from eyesore to eye-opener.

One step at a time

On the following pages, we'll show how the owners got from before to after. Although every job has many different challenges, there are some common denominators to be aware of in planning your new bath. The case study examined in this chapter covers the four main stages of bath construction: demolition, framing wet walls, rough plumbing, and finishing—closing in walls and setting fixtures.

Before getting down to work, make sure you have a well-designed plan based on a realistic look at your budget and your family's needs. Consider what work you are not only skilled to do, but have the time to do. Then review potential contractors carefully and check references before making your selection. Finally, keep in mind the golden rule of remodeling: Always expect the unexpected!

DEMOLITION

If you're eager to save money, consider doing demolition work yourself. It's one of two stages that an ambitious, semiskilled homeowner might want to tackle. (To learn about the other stage—setting fixtures—see pages 102 and 103.) As the word implies, demolition is a messy, dusty task. But if you follow procedures basic to plumbing and construction work while removing old walls and fixtures, you'll have fewer problems.

Obviously, you can't just whirl into a bath and start destroying everything in sight. This stage should be as orderly as any other. You need to first shut off the water; then take out freestanding fixtures; and finally, remove tile, tub, and flooring.

Removing lavatories

Procedures for removing a lavatory vary somewhat, depending upon whether yours is wall-hung or set into a counter top. With either type, you first shut off water to the fixture, disconnect supply lines to the faucet or faucets, and then remove the drain trap. Supply lines connect up underneath the basin with a pair of coupling nuts; many have a second set of connections down below, where water lines exit from the wall. (There may be shutoff valves located there, as well.)

Before you remove the trap, set a bucket underneath to catch water standing in the trap. Then loosen slip nuts at one or both ends of the trap and twist them loose. If you plan to reuse the trap, wrap the jaws of your wrench so you don't mar the plated finish.

Now you're ready to remove the basin, a job you may need help with. If your lavatory is wall-hung (it may also be supported with legs in front), it rests on a bracket or cleat at the rear, where it also may be secured with a couple of bolts. Loosen the bolts, if any, then simply lift the unit free. If your lavatory has legs, have someone on hand to catch them as they fall away.

In a counter-top installation, lay a length of 2x4 across the basin, with ends resting on either side of the counter. Next wrap a piece of wire around the 2x4, drop the wire down through the drain outlet, and wrap it around a second piece of wood underneath. Now unscrew the bolts that secure the rim to the counter's underside. Cutting or untwisting the wire lets you free the basin from the counter top.

After you've removed a lavatory, stuff a rag into the open line to keep sewer gas out of the house. If your fixture doesn't have shutoff valves, be sure the supply lines are capped off.

Removing the toilet

Again, shut off the water first. Flush the toilet and sponge out any water that remains in the bottom of the tank. Disconnect the supply line. If the tank is mounted on the bowl, remove the two bolts holding it in place under the rear rim of the bowl. Lift the tank off the bowl.

If the tank is mounted on the wall, remove the L-shaped spud pipe securing the tank to the bowl by removing slip nuts at either end of the pipe. Inside the tank you'll find bolts that hold the tank to the wall. Remove these and take away the tank.

Now look at the base of the bowl, and you'll find metal or ceramic caps covering bolts that secure the bowl to a flange on the floor. Remove the caps and bolts, rock the bowl gently to break a wax seal underneath, and lift the bowl free. Again, stuff rags into the drain pipe.

Removing the tub

You can break apart cast-iron tubs, like the one shown *at left*, with a sledge, but lighter steel tubs have to be removed in one piece. If the door isn't wide enough, you'll have to open a wall at one end and slide it out.

Your first task is to get at the tub's plumbing connections.

These may be accessible through a panel on the other side of the wall; if not, you'll have to cut a hole in the wall.

Once you have access to the connection, loosen the slip nuts that hold together the drain, trap, and overflow tube, and remove these components. Next, unscrew the spout by inserting the head of a pair of pliers into the spout opening and turning. Now attack the faucets. An exposed screw, or one covered with a decorative cap, lets you remove each handle and the decorative, cone-shaped cover underneath. Removing the big nuts threaded onto the faucet body lets you pull it out from behind.

After you've removed the fittings, chip out the tile to get at a flange that runs around the tub's perimeter. With a steel tub, this flange will be nailed or screwed to the wall studs; remove these fasteners, raise the tub, and slide it out on planks. Heavier cast-iron tubs simply rest in place and are not secured to studs.

Removing the walls and flooring

If possible, don't remove a bearing wall, one that helps hold up your house. To learn if a wall is bearing, check with a professional contractor.

Prior to taking out any wall, turn off the power. Remove tile, plaster, or drywall using a hammer, wrecking bar, and handsaw. Repeat on the other side of the studs. Cut the studs in two and pry away from the sole- and top plates. Then remove the end studs and plates.

Break loose tile flooring by whacking it with a heavy hammer or sledge, then slice it from the subflooring with a garden spade.

DEALING
WITH
THE MESS

DEALING WITH THE MESS

Organization and good humor may be the two most desirable qualities you bring to any remodeling project. They're even more valuable when the bathroom's involved. Inevitably, remodeling a bathroom will disrupt the entire family. If you can efficiently handle the mess, you'll help keep the level of stress down, and the job running smoothly.

The first step is to clean out the entire area, removing all furniture, carpets, and accessories. Also clear a path to the nearest exit, so you and the workers will be able to move materials in and out easily. Don't try to work around your belongings—that may cause needless damage and delays.

Next, hang sheets or plastic over adjacent doors and hallways. Tape the sheets to the door frames to prevent fine dust from drifting into other rooms when demolition is in progress. Wet the sheets to help keep dust down if you're removing plaster walls or ceilings.

Protect your floors with plastic, sheets, old carpets, or newspaper. Put a heavy-duty doormat at the outside exit.

Even with all these precautions, your house still will get dusty. That's where a sense of humor will help.

ROUGHING IN

"Roughing in" is the early stage of a plumbing job, when the supply, drain, and vent lines are run to their new locations. All work done afterward, including the setting of fixtures, is "finish" work. If you plan to do any roughing in yourself, get a copy of the local plumbing code, and be sure you understand how the plumbing in your house works. However, because this part of the project takes real skill and experience, most homeowners prefer to hire a licensed plumber for the job.

Before beginning, you'll need to obtain a permit from the local building department and arrange for inspections as the work progresses. Until you get approval, you can't cover up any new pipes.

In our sample remodeling *below, right*, the main challenge was to re-route the plumbing for the new lavatory and toilet. In the floor plan for the old bath *below, left*, the lavatory stood on the wall to the right of the door, with the toilet to the left. The new plan shifted the toilet to the right of the door. Workers bumped out the left wall into the adjoining closet space to make room for the lavatory and then put up two new "wet walls"—walls containing plumbing—to serve the fixtures. They also replaced the tub but didn't have to change the plumbing because the location was the same.

Every bath has two distinct water systems—one to supply water and the other to get rid of wastes (called the drain-waste-vent, or DWV, system). Obviously, it's essential they be kept separate from each other to avoid possible contamination of the water supply. Running new supply lines through existing 4-inch walls is relatively simple, but the DWV lines can be tricky. Because they carry away waste, water, and potentially poisonous sewer gases, they're thicker than supply lines and must *always* flow down, with little bending in them.

The water supply system begins where the main supply pipe enters your home. It then forks, one branch taking water to the water heater, the other carrying cold water. The two pipes, hot and cold, eventually go into a wall and are routed to the bath where they again branch to supply each fixture.

PLUMBERS' LANGUAGE

Drain-waste-vent (DWV) system Pipes that carry liquid and solid wastes to the sewer or septic tank and allow sewer gases to pass to the outside.
Main drain That part of the DWV system between the fixture drains and sewer drain.
Run Any length of pipe or fittings in a straight line.
Soil stack Vertical drain pipe carrying wastes to the sewer drain.
Trap Part of the fixture

drain that prevents sewer gases from entering the house.
Uniform Plumbing Code Nationally recognized set of guidelines prescribing safe plumbing practices.
Vent stack Upper part of a vertical drain line through which gases pass directly to the outside.
Wet wall Usually a 2x6 wall cavity housing the main drain/vent stack and a cluster of supply and DWV lines.

In this bath, providing new supply lines for the lavatory and toilet began with capping the old lines, then routing new pipes from the main hot and cold supply lines to the new wet walls. As shown *opposite*, wet walls are usually built with 2x6s to accommodate a 3- or 4-inch-diameter stack.

The key feature of the drain system in the bath is the large pipe that runs from the toilet to the ground where it connects into either a septic tank or sewage system. The vent stack is an extension of this drain pipe that runs up through the roof, allowing gas to escape. The soil stack, however, mainly determines how economically a bath can be remodeled. It's much simpler and cheaper to leave the toilet in its original spot. But as this remodeling project demonstrates, you can move the DWV stack if need be. The remodelers removed part of the floor and installed a new stack, tying it into the drain system in the basement. If possible, avoid running drains through joists because the large cuts required to do the job weaken the wood. If you must cut or notch any part of the structure, reinforce it adequately.

BEFORE　　　　　　**AFTER**

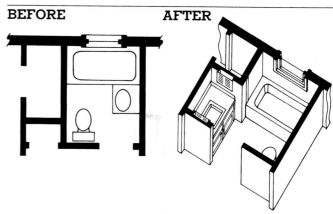

CLOSING UP THE WALLS

Now comes the best part—the finishing stage. With new wet walls built, pipes installed, and inspections passed, you can close up the walls and set the new fixtures. Most homeowners can tackle both tasks, although they are time-consuming and require careful execution.

The new pipes are connected, and the framing for new walls is in place. Once the plumbing inspector gives you the OK to "cover," the next step is closing up the bare studs.

The material for this job is drywall, but not the water-absorbing gray kind covering most walls and ceilings. Use a special type designed specifically for rooms like baths and kitchens. Unlike the surface of typical drywall, this "greenboard"—so called due to its color—is water-resistant and very durable. In addition, an asphalt-saturated inner core allows the whole board to stay rigid and dry.

However, actually working with greenboard is like working with other types of drywall. It is scored, snapped, and cut in the same fashion. The highest hurdles to clear are cutting and fitting around pipes—tricky jobs at best. And because most bathrooms are fairly small, with many corners and angles, they become even more difficult.

Greenboard is also heavier than standard drywall and therefore requires extra nailing. Nail at 6-inch intervals, spacing studs on 16-inch centers to handle the extra weight.

If the studs are more widely spaced, add a 2x4 support horizontally between each pair along the wall. Nail the greenboard to the supports and studs. To complete the job, tape, apply joint compound, and finish. If you like, apply tile, wallpaper, or wood paneling.

SETTING FIXTURES

The final step, and also the easiest, is connecting the new fixtures. Put them in after finishing the walls and floors, with the exception of the bathtub. If you're replacing it, do so *before* closing up.

Setting a tub
Connect all supply and drain lines and install the faucet body before moving the tub. Two people can move a steel or fiber-glass bathtub into position, but for a heavier, cast-iron tub, you'll need at least four strong bodies. Lay 2x4 runners on the floor—they'll act as skids—and push the tub into the framed enclosure. The flanges will rest atop vertical supports. A cast-iron tub weighs enough to anchor itself, but enameled steel and fiber-glass tubs should be nailed through the flanges to the studs. Install greenboard so it rests on the flange in such a way that tile or other finish material will meet the tub's rim.

Connect the drain assembly, checking for leaks in the supply and drain connections. Then apply silicone caulk around all openings and between the wall and tub to create a tight seal against moisture. Finally, install the tub spout, faucet handles and trim, and the shower arm and head.

Installing the toilet
Compared to most plumbing jobs, installing the toilet is easy—that is, once the supply and drain lines are in place. Begin by installing a closet flange (making sure the bolt slots are parallel to the wall), then insert the bowl's hold-down bolts that come with the toilet.

If your system has plastic pipe, apply solvent to the outside of the closet bend and the inside of the closet flange. Then fit the flange down onto the bend, twisting slightly to spread the solvent. Insert screws to secure the flange to the floor.

If your plumbing system has lead pipe, cut the pipe down to floor level and fit a brass flange over it, forming the lead so it lies back against the flange. Clean the joint, apply flux, and solder, aiming the torch at the flange, not the lead. Then screw the flange to the floor.

Next, run a bead of plumber's putty around the base of the bowl and fit a wax gasket over the outlet opening. Set the bowl upright and carefully place it atop the closet flange. The hold-down bolts should align with the holes in the base of the bowl. Then put a metal washer over each bolt, apply nuts, and tighten, being careful not to tighten so much that you crack the bowl.

To install the tank, place the spud washer, beveled edge down, over the bowl inlet opening. The washer forms the seal between the tank and bowl. Gently lower the tank onto the bowl, lining up the tank's holes with those at the rear of the bowl. Then secure the tank to the bowl with hold-down bolts, washers, and nuts. (Note that to prevent leaking, the rubber washer rests inside the tank under the bolt.)

Hook up the water supply line, and fasten the toilet seat in place. Finally, open the stop valve, fill the tank with water, flush the toilet, and check for leaks.

Installing lavatories
Most lavatories are the deck-mount, or counter-top, variety. To install one in a new counter

top, you have to cut a hole. First, trace the outline of the opening. With a self-rimming fixture, use the template provided. For a flush-mounted lavatory, position the rim securely, then trace around its outside edge. Cut with a saber saw.

Make all the faucet and drain assembly hookups. Run plumber's putty around the basin outlet. Insert the flange, then connect the gasket, drain body, and tailpiece.

To set a self-rimming fixture, run a bead of silicone adhesive around the flange's underside, about ¼ inch from the edge. Turn the fixture right side up and lower into the opening, aligning it carefully. Press down on the caulk, wiping off any excess.

To set a rim-type fixture, fasten the rim to the lavatory, set the sink into the opening, and secure with lugs spaced at 6- to 8-inch intervals. Secure the lugs with a screwdriver, then hook up the water lines and drain.

A wall-mounted lavatory
Before you close up the wall, cut a 2x10 to span the distance between the studs flanking the pipes. Then nail the 2x10 between the studs about 35 inches from the floor. After greenboard is up, screw the lavatory's hanger bracket to the 2x10 block, then check to make sure it's level. Turn the lavatory on its side, hook up the faucet and drain body, and lower the fixture onto the bracket. The flange on the bracket should fit into the corresponding slot in the lavatory. Connect water supply inlets to the stop valves, drain body, and drainpipe. Run water into the basin and check for leaks.

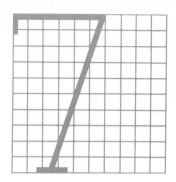

TREAT YOURSELF TO A SUPER BATH

No longer must every bath be a tiny, utilitarian room you hurry in and out of. Platform tubs, sunken tubs, hot tubs, whirlpools, saunas, and other splashy ideas offer relaxing incentives to stay awhile. If you're tempted to pamper your family with an aquatic delight, read on. This chapter tells what you need to know about nearly a dozen of bathing's nice-to-haves.

There's something sensuous about bathing in a sunken tub. You enter as if stepping into a tropical pool, slowly immersing your body—preferably up to the neck—and settling back to savor water's restorative effects. Even children can't wait to get into the suds.

Be warned, though, that tubs sunk flush with floor level pose a couple of problems: You need to find space under the floor for the tub and its drain fittings, and unless you provide a railing, someone could inadvertently step into what amounts to a gaping hole in the floor.

The oversized tub *opposite* solves both problems. It sits on an 8x8-foot platform at one end of an 8x14-foot master bath. A skylight helps to brighten the windowless room. In the background, translucent *shoji* screens also filter light into the bath from an adjacent glass-walled hallway. Large plants make the area even more inviting. Yet despite the light and open feeling, the whole room is satisfyingly private.

Interested in taking a bath like this? If so, you can design your room in many different ways. If your bathroom's on the ground floor, you may be able to sink a tub into a crawl space under the floor. On a second story, you might try dipping it into unused space over a garage or stairwell, or simply raise it up with a platform.

To get extra room for an especially large tub, consider expanding into an adjacent bedroom or closet. In any event, be sure the tub will fit through the doors of your house. Or if you're remodeling a bath, have it delivered through the incomplete walls of the new room.

Check weight

You may need to beef up floor joists for a very heavy tub. Ask a contractor or plumber to check. Even though the weight of an oversized tub—including the water and people in it—will be spread over a larger part of the floor, thus more evenly distributing the pressure, it's still a wise idea to ask for a professional opinion.

To give you an idea of just how weighty this issue is, a standard 5-foot iron tub tips the scales at about 500 pounds; a 6-foot tub, up to 700 pounds. If you put in 50 gallons of water to get a nice, deep soak (about 400 pounds) and add a 200-pound adult, the total is a hefty 1,100 to 1,300 pounds—more than a half-ton.

On the lighter side, a 6-foot plastic tub reinforced with fiber glass weighs only 170 pounds. Some manufacturers, however, expect lightweight tubs to be installed on a base of plaster or concrete. If so, the total weight will go up; plus, you'll need extra professional help.

Other kinds of plastic tubs are supported in a platform built with 2x4s, which spread the weight of the tub and water over the entire platform area, rather than just under the tub.

The platform itself can have two shallow ledges, as this one does, or two ordinary steps. Don't, however, place the steps right at the edge of the tub. In addition, installing a grab bar or two will make it easier and safer for bathers to enter and exit. (In fact, supervising children while they're bathing is not a bad idea.) Finally, flooring around the tub should have adequate traction.

BED AND BATH COMBINATIONS

In some new master suites, the walls are tumbling down—between the bedroom and bathroom. Why give up the partitions? For greater decorating versatility. Without sacrificing personal privacy, you can inject a luxurious sense of openness into areas that are typically small. If mixing porcelain with bedroom decor creates too much openness, you can easily isolate just the toilet—and maybe the shower—in a bed and bath combo. Finally, easy-to-maneuver room dividers can provide enough privacy for bathing in a room already secluded from the rest of the house.

Bed-bath combinations are a sweet place to wake up in and an equally pleasant spot to call it a day. If you remove the expected partitions between bathroom and bedroom, the resulting space takes on an unexpectedly dramatic appearance.

The suite *opposite* and *at right* capitalizes on a subdued color scheme of silvery gray, with accents of red and black to give the room a spacious, yet unified, look. Thick, humidity-resistant carpet helps muffle the sound of running water.

A private sitting room is at one end of the L-shaped floor plan *below* and next to the bed area, which is raised two steps to create a feeling of separation. A vanity counter *at right*, backed by a wall of freestanding storage units, further divides bed and bath areas.

The black bathtub *opposite* —on its own platform of black tile—is around the corner from the vanity. Exposed pipes sparkle next to the similarly dazzling claw-foot legs of the tub. The dressing area, toilet, and shower are partitioned off, as shown in the plan.

If you don't want a storage wall to shield the bathtub, try using a folding screen and separate lighting instead. That way, if one person goes to bed earlier or later than the other, the light the bather needs won't disturb the sleepyhead.

GARDEN BATHS

Looking for an area in your house to turn into a garden spot? Why not the bath? A green room makes for some enchanted bathing—and an exquisite place to relax naturally. Most plants thrive in the warm moist air, and most bathroom surfaces—ceramic tile, paneling, and glass—are tough enough to serve as pleasant mini-greenhouses.

The bath *above* is a real eye-opener. Glossy, black ceramic tile on walls, floors, and sunken tub contrast sharply with the natural green. A slanted glass wall admits plenty of sunlight and offers an attractive view of the trees outside. Inside, the plants provide privacy for the bather. In addition, a hand-held shower (not pictured) comes in handy for watering plants.

Cleaning the garden bath is easy. Any spills or mud splashed on the tiles after watering rinse away quickly. Moreover, the potted plants can be moved easily to other locations when they're not in bloom.

The tub platform made of tile *opposite* fits imaginatively into a space not much larger than the usual 5x8-foot cubicle. Placing the tub on a diagonal creates space for three planters made of redwood, the same material used to panel the walls. A skylight and large

clerestory window flood the area with plenty of sunlight for the plants; the variegated blue tile helps to set off their foliage and flowers.

When furnishing any garden bath, keep safety in mind. Place potted plants well back from the entrance to the tub. (For more information on adding plants to a bath, see pages 38 and 39.)

FACTS OF ARTIFICIAL LIGHT

Naturally, plants need light, but it doesn't have to come from the sun. Artificial light can work just as well. Here are some tips for planning your lighting needs:

• If your plants get any natural light, grow lights (special fluorescent tubes or incandescent bulbs) aren't necessary. Simply augment the real thing with light from ordinary fluorescent lights or incandescent bulbs.

• If the sun doesn't shine in, plants require special help. Grow lights give it to them by providing the red and blue wavelengths plants must have to grow properly. Grow lights may seem to be dimmer than ordinary bulbs or tubes, and their glow is a strange pinkish or bluish tone. But plants thrive under them.

• How much is enough depends on how much natural light the plant ordinarily needs. If it requires only low levels, then the plant will do nicely at 3 feet from a 40-watt fluorescent light or 100-watt incandescent bulb. If high levels are necessary, plants should be 1 foot from a 40-watt fluorescent source or 3 feet from a 300-watt incandescent bulb, but never closer than 2 feet—the heat may burn the foliage.

• Most plants don't require more than 15 hours of light a day.

TREAT YOURSELF TO A SUPER BATH

HOT TUBS AND SPAS

Hot tubs and spas are purely entertaining ways to stay healthy. Although each is made of different materials (wood and fiber-glass reinforced plastic, respectively), both tickle and soothe your body with hot, bubbly, filtered, constantly recirculating water. Often installed outdoors, spas and hot tubs may also be placed indoors for year-round pleasure—if your floor is (or can be made) strong enough to support a very heavy load.

The sturdy wooden hot tub pictured *opposite* was originally a brewery barrel. But you don't have to go into the beer business to find a tub. You can buy one especially designed for soaking; some even come in kits you can assemble yourself (for more on this, see page 112).

The main difference between hot tubs and spas, besides the material, is the way they stand up to the world. A wooden hot tub is self-supporting. A plastic spa, however, is a lightweight, contoured shell that must be supported around its edge by a deck or frame, or be buried in the ground outdoors.

Hot tubs are weighty propositions. Make sure a contractor reinforces the floor so it can support the combined weight of wood and water (up to 1,000 gallons, at approximately 8 pounds per gallon). In addition, allow for enough space around the tub so you can enter it easily from the sides. Hot tubs range from 4 to 8 feet in diameter and most are about 4 feet deep. (A few square models are on the market.) Nearly all tubs are made of redwood, but you'll also find cedar, cypress, mahogany, teak, and oak.

A fiber-glass spa should be trim and neat. If it's well made, all the edges will be of an even thickness, free of hairline cracks or creases. At the same time, the best designs have reinforcing across the bottom of the spa, around all the outlets, and at the steps.

Technically speaking

Tubs and spas come fitted with plumbing and heating units that run either on electricity or natural or bottled gas. Before choosing, consider the cost of these fuels in your area. You'll also need a filtra-tion system, along with controls for it and a connection to the drainpipe.

Place the controls where you can reach them easily—in the basement, perhaps, or in a nearby closet.

Be sure that all the accessories (filter, pump, heater) are the right size for the model you select. Remember, too, that tubs with hydromassage units need larger pumps than those that merely recirculate water.

Before buying, inquire if the pump needs 220-volt wiring. For safety's sake, ask a professional to supervise electrical and plumbing hookups.

Water, water everywhere

You'll need to check the purity of the water periodically and add correctives. To do this adequately, a testing kit is essential. And even though the water recirculates, it's best to drain the tub every month or two and clean it thoroughly.

Because a tub or spa is a source of heat and humidity, the room it's in should have vapor barriers on the walls, ceiling, and floor, plus multiple glazing on windows and skylights to control condensation. You'll need a good ventilation system, too. In addition, you may want to buy an insulated cover for the tub; it will retain heat in the water and keep your energy bills as low as possible.

If you have a wooden tub, be prepared for a little leakage the first few days, before the staves absorb enough water to tighten against the metal hoops on the outside.

One more point. Tannin in the wood will leach into the water the first time you fill the tub, turning the water a light brown. Don't worry about it. The leaching is not harmful and ends quickly.

TAKING THE HEAT— SAFELY

High heat stresses your body. Some safety rules to follow for hot tubs and spas, as well as for saunas or steam baths, are given below.
• Don't try to take extreme heat if you have diabetes or circulatory problems (including heart troubles). Your body may have difficulty withstanding it.
• Don't drink. Both alcohol and heat expand blood vessels. Together they cause too much strain. In any case, you don't want to become drowsy while sitting in deep water.
• Use the buddy system. If one person gets into trouble, the other can help or get aid.
• Don't go into the water with a full stomach. Wait an hour or two.
• Until your body builds up some tolerance to the heated water, limit your stays to about 20 minutes.
• Never let the water temperature exceed 104° F. For children under five years old, keep the water under 98° F.
• Don't settle into a hot tub, steam room, or sauna directly after heavy exercise. Allow your body to cool down first. Similarly, do not *follow* with heavy exercise.
• Make sure children have adult supervision. Provide a safe way to climb in and out.

HOT TUB BASICS

ANATOLY OF A HOT TUB SYSTEM

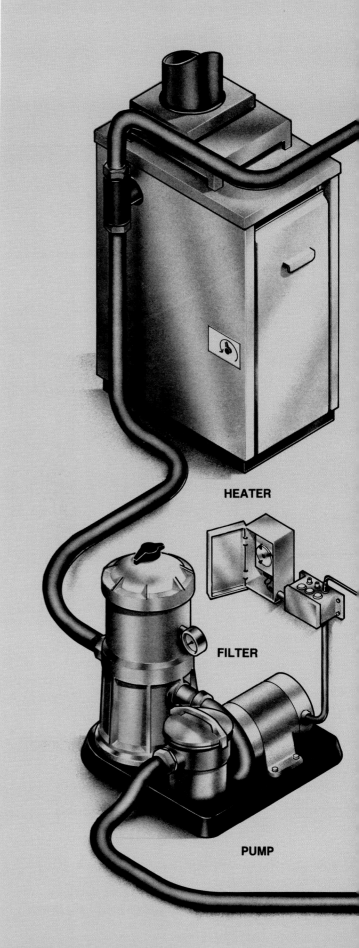

HEATER

FILTER

PUMP

Hankering for a hot tub? If so, do some research about its construction before you get in over your head. Each tub is a complex system made up of the tub itself, and the filter, heater, and pump. Although many manufacturers choose components and sell the whole system as a unit, it pays to know something about the individual parts. You then may be able to build a hot tub from scratch, tailoring it to your own particular needs.

To help you become more familiar with hot tubs, we've described *below* the functions of the four major components.

• *The tub.* In the beginning, many tubs were refurbished wine tanks. Today, most still look as though they've come directly from a winemaker's cellar, with round or oval sides made of beveled staves that are secured by metal hoops and a dado joint at the sides. Generally, sturdy joists support the bottoms and rest on a solid layer of concrete or a similarly reinforced material.

Why all the support? The average tub is 4 feet deep and 5 to 6 feet in diameter. Add 500 to 700 gallons of water, three to five bathers, and the total weight approaches 4 tons.

Redwood is the most common material used to make tubs, but cedar, cypress, oak, and teak are equally good choices.

• *The filter.* Hot tubs recirculate water. By trapping solids, a filter keeps the water clear so it can be used again and again without being drained away. You'll find three kinds: cartridge filters, which are the least expensive; diatomaceous earth (DE) filters, which are the most costly; and sand filters, which are moderately expensive.

• *The heater.* It keeps the water constantly warm. You'll find a variety on the market— from models fueled by natural gas, propane, or heating oil, to electric versions. Performance and price vary considerably.

• *The pump.* It's the prime mover, pushing water through the filter and heater into the tub. A pump's capacity must be matched closely to those of the filter and heater. Hydrojets and blowers are separate parts that produce the water's swirling and bubbling.

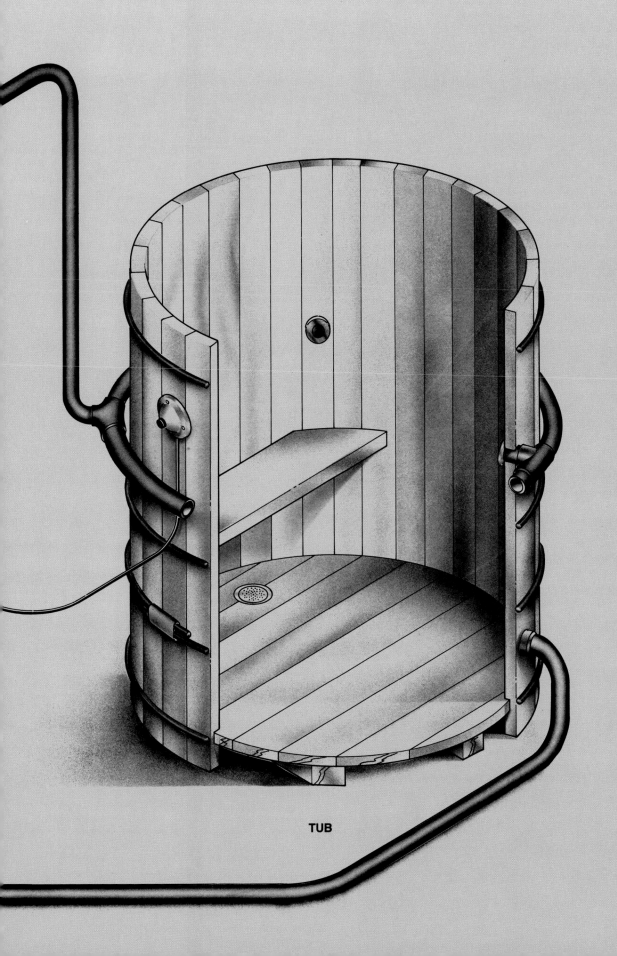

TUB

SOAKING TUBS

Relaxing in hot water up to your neck is a time-honored therapeutic tradition. (The Japanese have been doing it for centuries.) They prefer wooden tubs, but in this country, plastic tubs reinforced with fiber glass are more common, as are custom-made tubs surfaced in ceramic tile. Traditionalists take a shower before entering a soaking tub to relax, so the water can be used again. Others prefer to soak and soap in the same sequence, draining the water after each use. Take your choice.

The bright orange tub shown *above* beckons the weary body. Nestled between a vanity and open shelves for storing towels, this bath features a molded built-in bench under the waterline. Wide steps covered in tile make climbing in and out easy and also double as convenient spots to dry off. In addition, the materials used to construct the walls and floor complement each other so the tub doesn't seem out of place or conspicuous. An overhead heat lamp warms bathers when they step out of the tub.

Tubs like this can be installed above floor level, partially below it, or completely below it. In any case, be sure to reinforce the joists: Filled to the top, the tub *above* weighs 600 pounds—without anybody in it.

The tub *opposite* is made of vivid blue tile, with a mosaic of fish and flowers covering the bottom and sides. Measuring 4x5 feet, and 2 feet deep, it's enclosed in redwood and has a bench on two sides. Redwood applied diagonally halfway up the wall resists steam and soapsuds.

To supply a soaking tub, you may need an extra large water heater—or even a separate heater just for the tub. In either case, a ¾-inch water line will fill the tub faster. And before installing any tub, check the clearance needed to get it into the room. (The tiled tub, of course, was custom-built just for this bath.)

TREAT YOURSELF TO A SUPER BATH

WHIRLPOOL AND STEAM BATHS

If your feathers get ruffled by the hassles of daily living, try turning the bath into a delightful oasis. A whirlpool or steam bath will water you down and cheer you up. With equipment available today, you can either add one to your present bath or install it when you're remodeling.

The feathered friend *at right* is enjoying the soothing agitation of a whirlpool bath. You can, too, with either a portable clamp-on unit for your present tub, or an entirely new tub with built-in sockets for air and water jets. Some portable electric machines, using ½-horsepower motors, move 50 gallons of water a minute—more than enough to massage and loosen tight muscles. Once you're through, simply store the portable whirlpool in a closet until you're ready to use it again. (Cordless, battery-operated portable units are also available.)

If you're looking for a more permanent arrangement, you may rather have a whirlpool bathtub. Different sizes are available that can hold one or two people.

Before buying one, however, consider the weight of the tub, water (approximately 8 pounds per gallon), and surrounding platform. Large tubs can be as long as 6 or 7 feet and up to 5 feet wide, compared to a standard tub that's 5 feet long and 32 inches wide. Check the strength of the floor supports before installing either size.

Because you fill and drain whirlpool tubs (instead of using filtered and recirculated water), speed becomes an important question. As with other kinds of units, you may want to install ¾-inch waterlines rather than the usual ½-inch lines, so you can fill the tub twice as fast and so the water won't cool off by the time the tub is full. Doing this, however, will make installation more expensive.

Again, as with other kinds of tubs, the water heater must be large enough to handle the demand; one that's double the normal size—or a separate heater just for the whirlpool itself—usually works best. Also, look for a water heater with a high recovery rate, say 160 gallons per hour for an 80-gallon tank. Large tubs made for two hold as much as 150 gallons at a time. To work well, they should contain at least a foot of water.

Getting steamed

Another healthy way to relax at home is to take a steam bath. It's good for the sinuses, helps loosen tight muscles, and also increases the flow of blood and supply of oxygen to the body's tissues.

There are various kinds. One steam bath is essentially a small cabinet (you've probably seen it in old movies with a person sitting inside, head sticking out). In fact, it doesn't need to be in the bath at all and fits into nearly any alcove; just plug it into a standard 110-volt receptacle.

A simple steam bath attachment connects to the shower outlet pipe, generating steam from the hot water running into it. Installing one requires no electrical or plumbing work.

If you want to get a little more steamed in your bath, you can add actual steam-generating capability to the shower or tub enclosure, once you've enclosed it with a ceiling panel. The steam generator itself can be outside the bathroom, so it doesn't eat into precious space there. The unit requires a 220-volt electrical line, a supply line for cold water, and a ½-inch copper or brass steam line running to the steam outlet in the enclosure. A timer automatically cuts off steam at a predetermined interval.

TREAT YOURSELF TO A SUPER BATH

SAUNAS

The image of the rigorous Finnish sauna is more fearsome than the reality is. Only old-world devotees are likely to beat themselves with birch twigs or follow the dry heat treatment with a plunge into a snowbank or cold stream. Less hearty newcomers to the tradition find that spending time in the dry heat of a sauna, and alternating with a lukewarm shower and rest, proves both exhilarating and relaxing.

Sweating it out in a sauna stimulates the circulation, rids the body of toxins, and leaves your skin glowing. Dry heat (160 to 220 degrees Fahrenheit at 10 to 30 percent humidity) promotes rapid perspiration that evaporates almost immediately. Following the sauna with a shower and a brisk rubdown helps to remove dead layers of skin and leaves you squeaky clean.

A family seriously committed to staying fit designed the sauna *opposite*. They incorporated the prefabricated unit into a niche off a large master bath. For them, it's easy to take a sauna, move to the shower (out of camera range), then weigh in on the scale next to the sauna door.

Sauna steps

• Before entering, remove your watch, glasses, and all jewelry. They'll get too hot to bear.
• Dress as informally as you like—wear a towel or bathing suit, or nothing at all.
• Once in, relax on a bench. Take it easy at first. Stay in only as long as you feel comfortable; at the beginning, ten minutes may be a good maximum time. As you get more accustomed to the heat, move to the higher benches, which are hotter.
• Get out after ten to 30 minutes. Take a cooling shower and a short rest before returning for a second round of heat. Pour a small amount of water onto the peridotite rocks over the stove (peridotite is a dark igneous rock). This will increase the humidity slightly and promote additional sweating. Just a little bit will do: too much and the room will become oppressive.

• Take another brief shower, cool off, and head into the sauna one more time. Afterward, take a soapy shower to clean off.

The whole process takes little more than an hour, and you'll emerge feeling totally restored.

Some people skip the return trips and just stay in for one session, then take a shower. Whatever pattern you choose, don't follow the sauna with a soak in a hot tub. Your body will build up too much heat.

Also, drink plenty of water before and after you take a sauna to replace what you've lost in sweating. (For other health precautions, see page 110.)

Sauna basics

The size of a sauna depends on how many people will use it at once. Plan one or two levels of benches long enough for an adult to stretch out on.

Smaller saunas that fit one or two people can easily be built into a large closet or two small back-to-back closets combined. Freestanding sheds also make good spots, especially for larger saunas.

For convenience's sake, locate a sauna near a shower, with a place to lie down close by. If you wish, include skylights for a more open feeling.

The benches, usually 24 inches wide, are 18 and 36 inches high. For other building details, see the box *below*.

SAUNA SPECIFICS

You can build a sauna from a kit or design one yourself. Sizes range from 28x42x78 *inches* to 8x10x7 *feet*. Manufacturers even produce a "door-kit" to convert a closet into a sauna. The door contains all the necessary features of a sauna. All you have to do is insulate the closet and add a bench. For places to buy kits, check the Yellow Pages.

If you plan to build one yourself, keep a few tips in mind. The walls of a sauna consist of ordinary stud-wall construction. Doors should be solid-core wood or insulated. Windows need to be double-glazed. Use foil-faced mineral batt insulation between studs and joists, with an air space so heat can reflect between the foil and interior paneling. Or use mineral insulation with a continuous vapor barrier of aluminum foil over the insulation and studs and under the paneling.

Walls, ceiling, and benches should be well-seasoned wood and free of knots. Aspen, pine, and redwood are common choices. To prevent burns, inset or conceal nails, and as an added precaution, build a wood rail around the metal stove. The floor can be ceramic tile, vinyl, or concrete, covered with wood slats.

Gas or electric sauna heaters work faster than wood-burning heaters. With an electric system, you won't need outside plumbing or ventilation. Most units require 220-volt wiring; some small ones operate on 110 volts. Unlike electric heaters, gas and wood-burning heaters need an outside vent. To get adequate heat, the room needs about 3,000 BTUs or one kilowatt per 45 cubic feet of sauna space.

TREAT YOURSELF TO A SUPER BATH

EXERCISE CENTERS

In numbers never thought possible before, Americans are trying to get fit and stay fit. That's a good sign, but it also poses a problem: Just finding space in a crowded world of exercisers is sometimes a difficult chore. Well, look no further. An exercise center in your bedroom/bathroom may be the most convenient—and most effective—way to get a jump on the day or end it on the right foot. With a few modifications, your home can become a pleasurable place to work out.

With a little work and a lot of dedication, exercising at home may be the best program for you. If you plan to convert your bedroom/bathroom into a mini-gym, keep the following tips in mind.

● Provide adequate ventilation (but no cold drafts), and keep the temperature at a constant, comfortable level.

● Be sure you have the space to do exercises you enjoy.

● Buy and install easy-to-clean surfaces; be sure they're durable as well.

● In addition, make sure surfaces in the room are compatible with the exercises you want to do. Pirouetting on a throw rug, for example, is not a safe way to get in shape.

● Check to see that any equipment is properly installed. If your exercises require props, store them nearby.

● Decorate in bright colors; they're motivational perks to keep you exercising consistently. And make the decor in the exercise center as "energetic" as possible with wall hangings, posters, and other decorations to give you that psychological boost.

● Play music while you're exercising. The sound system doesn't have to be elaborate; just something to pep you up and keep you going.

● Use mirrors, not only to check on the results over time, but also to inspect the way you do certain exercises.

The exercise center *opposite* is a good example. Space is plentiful, without fragile or superfluous objects getting in the way. Mirrors enhance the sense of openness and give the exerciser a chance to see how the program is going. And the bed, upholstered in moisture-resistant fabric, is a satisfying place to take a break when the exercises are over.

HOW MUCH ROOM DO YOU NEED?

What's the smallest amount of space a piece of exercise equipment takes up? 1½x2½ feet! That's all the room a compact exercise bicycle occupies.

One person can easily pursue a substantial fitness program in an area as small as 4x10 feet. Two people can manage in 8x10 feet, without bumping into each other, although a more comfortable size for two is 15x15 feet. Of course, it all depends on the equipment you choose.

Here are some standard pieces of exercise equipment that may make good bedroom/ bathroom companions:

● Exercise mats vary in size from 2x6 feet to 5x10 feet.

● Slant boards are generally 6 feet long.

● An incline bench, the kind weight trainers use with dumbbells, is only 5 feet long. However, to use it properly, you'll need at least 6 feet of space on either side.

● A rowing machine measures 2x4 feet; you'll require, of course, extra elbowroom.

You can even fit a trampoline into an ordinary bedroom. A small "rebounder," about 3½ feet across, sits just off the floor and will bounce you only a few inches while you're exercising on it.

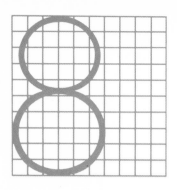

BATHROOM PROJECTS YOU CAN BUILD

You can make it if you try! Sometimes the answers to bothersome questions about a bath are right at your fingertips. This chapter describes a number of projects you can do on your own—installing vital new vanities, boxing in unattractive old fixtures, constructing handy storage units, and lighting up a bath like never before. Try one, two, or more. Each is designed to make your bath look and live better.

VANITIES

Vanities add valuable counter space to a bath. An out-of-the-way alcove is a perfect hideaway for the vintage washstand *above*. Placed in one corner of a bedroom, it offers an attractively private niche for overnight guests.

The oak washstand, with its unusual marble top, needed new plumbing. The owners chose china fittings that were in keeping with the old-fashioned look of the heavy wood cabinet and hand-painted basin.

The vanity *opposite* stretches along the entire wall with abundant storage below; excellent overhead lighting brightens the room.

The latticework framing the mirror, window, and storage compartments is made from prebuilt panels that come in 2x8-foot and 4x4-foot sections. Because they can't be cut to size (each strip is only 1/8 inch thick), using the standard panels is most efficient.

To build your own panels, however, use 1-inch boards for frames and nail lath strips to the back. Space them the width of one lath apart in a crisscross pattern. Nail strips going in one direction, then those going the other way.

VANITIES

(continued)

Tired of a bath dressed all in white? Add a little color using materials that take moisture with the best of them—redwood and canvas.

The vanity counters in the bath *at far right* are not the usual ho-hum variety. Made of durable redwood sections (as is the floor), both provide comfortable space in a less conventional way. In addition, the dark green, canvas-front cabinets provide good storage and colorfully cover up exposed pipes in the room.

The sturdy redwood shelving *near right* not only adds precious counter space to the bath, it also supports a handy towel rack made from leftover pieces of redwood and a dowel that's stained to match.

Like the floor, the wide shelf is put together with redwood patio sections (they're less expensive than planks), then topped with glass so cleaning isn't the chore it would otherwise be.

To install the towel rack, nail 2x4 cleats to the bottom of the shelf, as shown in the illustration *lower right*. Then screw the towel rack to the cleats.

Waterproof the shelf and towel rack with four coats of polyurethane, a finish you should apply to all redwood surfaces in a bath. Finish the job by using metal L brackets to attach the shelf to the wall.

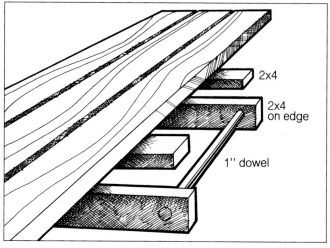

2x4

2x4
on edge

1'' dowel

BOXING IN FIXTURES

Most standard fixtures are set in their ways. Because they're not about to go anywhere, they sometimes present a perplexing decorating problem. Boxing them in can give old, immovable fixtures a custom look, provide extra storage and counter surfaces, and even fashion comfortable benches where you can sit down and leisurely towel off.

The four projects described on these two pages present different camouflages for standard fixtures. One of them may give you an idea for a whole new bath. (For more information on how to box in standard fixtures, see pages 34 and 35.)

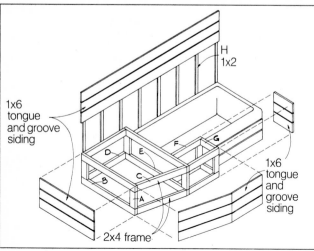

1x6 tongue and groove siding

H 1x2

D E F G
B C
A

2x4 frame

1x6 tongue and groove siding

This bath *upper left* has redwood built-ins on all sides. Before beginning, chart the entire project on graph paper. You'll need 2x4 and 1x2 lumber, 1x6 tongue-and-groove redwood or cedar siding, paneling adhesive, caulk, nails, polyurethane varnish, and plumbing accessories.

Assemble the frame for the deck from 2x4 verticals and crosspieces. Rough in necessary plumbing, then attach 1x2 furring strips to the wall.

Cover the deck and sides with 1x6 tongue-and-groove redwood or cedar, bedding the joints in caulk. If necessary, leave openings for plumbing fixtures. Miter boards to get a good fit; then use paneling adhesive to attach the siding directly to the sides of the tub. If your tub is curved, even out the surface using 1x2s and shims.

Next, nail siding to furring strips to cover the wall; then apply four coats of polyurethane. Complete plumbing installations, if necessary.

To finish, caulk edges of the siding and fixtures.

W ood isn't the only material you can use for boxing in standard fixtures. Tile is a natural, too. *At right*, the hand-painted imported tile around a painted ceramic sink creates an invigorating Mexican motif. The stucco finish on the plaster continues the south-of-the-border motif.

The same vivid tiles surrounding the sink form a border for the mirror. Both mirror and tiles are put up on a simple-to-install hardboard frame.

Other accessories are kept to a minimum and don't get in the way. Clear plastic shelves, a chrome light fixture over the mirror (not shown), the plastic towel rack, and the clear soap dish are hardly noticeable in this colorfully understated design.

R edwood and mahogany planks, protected by polyurethane, make the material difference in the bath *above*. The 4x5-foot, boxed-in tub platform doubles as an extra bench and as a place to drape towels and clothing. A boxed-in oval vanity has plenty of storage space.

Wood abounds elsewhere in the room. Panels of redwood strips frame the ceiling light over the vanity counter, and a built-in redwood towel rack (reflected in the mirror) runs the length of the bath.

P lastic laminate is yet another material you can choose. The trapezoid-shaped vanity cabinet in the bath *at left* uses it to sleek advantage. It adds a slightly unconventional touch to the slightly unconventional wedge-shaped basin.

To build the cabinet, carefully miter the corners of the wood frame, surface the sides with plywood, then apply the laminate. Set the basin into a precut hole in the top.

The bath is unusual in other ways, as well. Instead of the typical medicine cabinet and mirror behind the vanity, artwork is displayed on a wall surfaced with wood slats.

Shaving? That's handled by a pull-out swivel mirror, attached to the wall over the towel ring. It makes for a closer view and eliminates having to lean over the sink.

STORAGE

Part of a completely remodeled bath that measures only 6x8 feet, the old-fashioned cabinet *below* is a solid addition to the room's turn-of-the-century theme. It goes well with a pedestal sink and the striking clawfoot bathtub *opposite*, *lower right*.

Originally used to store medicine, the cabinet languished in a salvage yard until the owners picked it out. They stripped layer after layer of old paint, fitted the cabinet with a curved fir shelf, and mounted it into the wall. The towel rack at the left uses a 1-inch dowel.

To make a unit like this, insert a standard cabinet or shelving into stud space. Remove the old door, install a wooden frame, and then add a mirrored door with an old-fashioned pull.

The walls and ceiling have a novel look, as well (and not only because of the bare bulb in a plain ceramic socket). They're made of hemlock-beaded ceiling board, once a favorite material for porch ceilings. This updated version has a clear polyurethane finish to protect it from water.

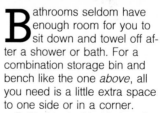

Bathrooms seldom have enough room for you to sit down and towel off after a shower or bath. For a combination storage bin and bench like the one *above*, all you need is a little extra space to one side or in a corner.

Built of teak, this bin-bench wraps around two walls of a remodeled bath. Sections of the seat lift up, uncovering space for towels, cleaning supplies, and other bathroom supplies.

To build a project like this, first size the bench to fit your own bathroom, selecting a comfortable height and depth.

Build a basic box with a frame of 2x4s, and attach the back of it to the wall. Cover the front with paneling.

Then divide the top into separate panels. Frame in each lid so it fits the bench snugly, cutting wood to fit the sections.

Finally, hinge the lids to the frame, and finish the job with a moisture-resistant finish.

Old-fashioned baths often have unused space at the end of the tub. And old-fashioned houses often lack a proper linen closet. The bath *below* is an example of how to solve both problems.

The simple towel "ladder" takes up little space but provides plenty of storage. You can add more shelves than are shown here or use the extra space to store a small stool or hamper.

To build the ladder, glue and dowel two pine 2x4s side-by-side. Support the shelves on dowels projecting through the side pieces into the ends of the shelves. (Note that all the shelves should stick out a bit in front and back. You can later use the dowels as hooks.)

Cut the uprights slightly shorter than the height of the ceiling. You'll need a little clearance to swing the unit up from the floor after it's assembled. When everything's ready, shim it into place for a tight, secure fit.

One other option is to use screw-in glides at the bottom that allow you to adjust the height of the ladder. They're especially helpful if you're trying to even out the shelves on an uneven floor.

(continued)

You don't need much space for the flip-top hamper *above*. Fit for any house, it's easy to clean under and, unlike wicker hampers, won't snag your clothing.

Just size it to the space available. But make sure to figure the angle cuts carefully to get a good, tight fit.

Using 3/4-inch interior plywood, cut the back and sides first, mitering the edges as necessary.

Glue and nail the back and sides together. Then outline a pattern for the top and bottom. Attach the bottom. Sink all nailheads and fill with wood putty.

For a durable surface, apply plastic laminate to the sides, top, and exposed edges. Or paint all the surfaces with an alkyd-based (oil-based) paint. Remember to paint inside surfaces as well.

When the finishing is complete and the paint is dry, attach the top, using two butt hinges or a piano hinge.

To attach the hamper to a wall, drill the holes first, and then screw from the inside of the hamper directly into at least two wall studs. If necessary, use toggle bolts for a more secure hold.

STORAGE

(continued)

Most baths have wasted space overhead. Give yours a lift—and brighten the room at the same time—by building and installing a wall-to-wall light-shelf like the one shown *at left*.

Begin with two lengths of 2x10s. Cut one piece 1½ inches shorter than the other. Hold the shorter piece in a vertical position, then nail and glue it to the back of the other piece so the completed assembly forms a right angle. This serves as the back of the shelf and shields the fluorescent light.

Now nail end boards, ¾ inch thick, to each end, extending them to the back wall. Sink all nailheads, and fill the recesses with wood putty.

Paint the entire shelf white or use another light color. If you prefer to stain the shelf and coat it with polyurethane or to paint it a darker color, it's still a good idea to paint the back white so it reflects more light into the room.

Mount the light fixture to the back of the shelf. If necessary, install wiring for the fixture adjacent to the shelf. Then lift the shelf into place and screw the end boards into the wall. Attach the entire unit to the wall studs, if possible. If not, use toggle bolts or expansion bolts to secure the shelf unit to the hollow wall.

Now it's time for the finishing touches. Counterbore the screwheads, fill with wood putty, and touch up with paint or stain and varnish, as necessary. Complete the wiring of the light fixture.

Note the simple ladder that doubles as towel rack and window treatment.

The space race in the bath is always hard to win, but the nifty, easy-to-build storage unit *at right* can help you come out on top. Shallow enough to fit handily into the small space near the door, it's a combination towel rack and medicine cabinet, with room below for a wicker storage basket or hamper.

Use ¾-inch plywood. The cabinet doors are ¼-inch tempered hardboard. Cut to size and paint the pieces any color you want.

Build the unit on the floor and slip it into place. Cut the uprights to length, making sure they're slightly shorter than the height of the ceiling so later you have enough room to swing the unit upright.

Drill holes in the uprights for the 1-inch dowels that make up the towel rack. Cut dadoes in the uprights and attach the top and bottom of the cabinet.

Next install plastic sliding-door tracks for the cabinet. Cut doors to size from ¼-inch tempered hardboard. Then position the top of the uprights, and slide the lower ends into place, shimming at the bottom, if necessary.

Using small angle irons, secure the unit to the wall. Then slip the sliding doors into place to finish the job.

Space is what you make of it, and the clever wooden towel cage *above* is an effective way to fill up a blank wall. (The shelving, constructed from cedar 1x2s, will age to a silvery-gray color.)

To build this project, you need eight crosspieces for each shelf and seven uprights for each side, plus two ledger boards. Use ⅜-inch or ½-inch dowels to pin everything together. (Buy extra doweling to allow for mis-cuts and to peg the unit to the wall.)

First clamp a number of 1x2s together so you can accurately drill holes for all the dowels at once. To assemble, lay the back crosspiece for each shelf on the floor and place two uprights at the ends. Dowel and glue the pieces together. Next, alternately slide crosspieces and uprights on the protruding dowels. Glue the last uprights and crosspieces to the dowels.

To support the shelving, use the 1x2 ledger boards, pegged to the wall below the top and bottom crosspieces. Equally effective supports are small, inconspicuous angle irons attached to the studs.

Baths should be as decorative as the rest of the house. The bath *above* is part of a traditional decorating scheme carried throughout this home's other rooms.

A shallow niche provides more than enough storage space for towels. Unlike those made of wood, which tend to warp, these shelves of white acrylic plastic stand up well to the bath's heat and humidity. You can purchase the stock track and brackets supporting these adjustable shelves in almost any hardware or department store.

The wainscoting is 1x6 tongue-and-groove car siding (wood originally used on the interior of railroad cars). Coated with semigloss enamel it is highly moisture-resistant. The molding comes from several different molding profiles available at most millworks or building supply stores.

Finally, the wooden shutter at the window completes the traditional, easy-to-live-with decor of this handsome bath.

LIGHTING

Lighting shouldn't be left till last. Plan it as an integral part of any remodeling.

Using skylights is one way to brighten the picture. The bath *below* is under the eaves of an attic and was once a narrow, 6x14-foot storage room. Two large skylights bring in plenty of sunlight. At night, an old-fashioned glass fixture over the door and a custom-made built-in over the recycled lavatory provide more than enough light.

The simple box surrounding the vanity light is made from redwood 1x8s, mounted on 1x4s like those in the wain-scoting. The medicine cabinet, recessed into the stud wall, is fronted by a mirror mounted on ½-inch plywood and framed with redwood 2x2s. This mirror and another oval mirror over the old bureau help bounce light around the room, as do the white ceiling and walls.

When remodeling or adding a bath, remember that skylights and clerestories can bring daylight into cramped rooms without filling the walls with windows. And old bath fixtures, combined with these modern structural features, exude a unique charm no completely new bath can duplicate.

Structural lighting that you build in is another remodeling option.

Above, a contemporary light fixture over the vanity uses a grillwork of fir 1x3s to shield the light and hide an overhead exhaust fan.

The narrow fir boards rest on a 1x1-inch ledge. When the fluorescent tubes in the light fixture need to be changed, it's easy to reach them by moving the fir boards aside.

The lighting and ventilation systems are boxed in to make the room look sleeker and to help lower a very high ceiling, bringing it more into scale with the 5x11-foot room. A re-cessed downlight, built into the lowered ceiling over the tub, brightens that area.

The tub enclosure has angular built-ins to disguise the old tub and provide storage and display space. In addition, the floor and top surfaces of the tub platform are made from the same ceramic tile. White tile continues from the built-ins right onto the walls. A long towel rack of oak 1x6s runs along the back and side walls.

If store-bought goods aren't for you, then *build* a light fixture that's the only one of its kind in your neighborhood. The light tube *below* consists of an aluminum irrigation pipe fitted with bulbs. Paint the tube with automotive lacquer to suit your bathroom decor.

The interior of the pipe is fitted with four 250-watt halogen bulbs that screw into standard sockets. The halogen variety lasts longer than an ordinary bulb, produces more light for its size, and doesn't distort skin tones.

Install the tube a foot or so below the ceiling, so the ceiling serves as a reflector. Cap the ends with wood blocks that you bolt or screw to the wall. Then fit as many bulbs as you want into the tube.

The tube light plugs into an ordinary wall socket that has been set high into the large mirror. Since the cord will show, highlight it by using a high-tech retractile type. Or if you'd rather hide the cord completely, install a receptacle at the end of the tube. Then the cord won't dangle over the side but will be hidden inside the trough.

Light fixtures that you purchase and install are an effective way to shed some light on your bath. The lighting sections of major department stores sell an amazing range of products, from the glamour of fancy fixtures to the simplicity of the bare-bulb look *above.*

Four "soft white" light bulbs high over the vanity illuminate one half of the room without causing any glare. The mirrored back wall of the alcove spreads the light around. A second mirror, at a right angle to the first, makes checking hairdos a cinch.

The white walls reflect light and set off the oak vanity that provides storage space. And the ceiling of fir 1x4s is a nice change from the old, humdrum white ceiling.

Finally, with these crisp basics, you can revise your color scheme at any time just by adding a new set of towels.

9

STOCKING YOUR BATH

Towels, grooming aids, accessories, soaps, and cleansers—it takes a heap of products to give your bath its own personality and tailor it for your family's needs. This chapter shows several dozen possibilities from among the hundreds of items you'll find in a bath shop and offers buymanship tips to help you get the best values for your money.

LINENS

Bath linens add style and color to a bath, but don't select them for appearance only. Consider absorbency and durability, as well. One hundred percent cotton towels are the most absorbent. When you check labels, though, you'll find that polyester is often added to increase wearability and reduce shrinkage. These benefits come at the cost of reduced absorbency, so with synthetic-blend towels, choose those that have polyester only in the base fabric; the looped pile surface should be all cotton.

Loop terry towels are more absorbent than sheared loop towels, which are labeled "velour." If you like the look of velour, choose linens with velour on one side and loop terry on the other.

Bath linens come in a wide array of colors, woven prints and patterns, and a variety of sizes. *Jacquard* patterns are woven into the towel and appear on both sides. Printed patterns are silk screened onto only one side; poor quality prints may fade after a short period of wear.

Machine wash bath linens in warm water and detergent. Be sure to wash dark-colored towels separately because they generally bleed for three to four launderings. Don't use fabric softeners with bath towels; these additives often contain silicones that make cotton fibers repel water.

Select your bath linens from these standard sizes:
Bath mitt (1) 6x10 inches
 and up
Tub mat (2) 22x36 inches
Hand towel (3) 16x30 inches
Wash cloth (4) 13x13 inches
Bath towel (5) 27x50 inches
Bath sheet (6) 36x70 inches
Guest towel (not shown)
 11x18 inches

GROOMING APPLIANCES

The devices shown here help you put your best face—or figure—forward, and can save you time and effort as well. For a modest cash outlay, grooming aids like these give professional results and help streamline bathroom routines.

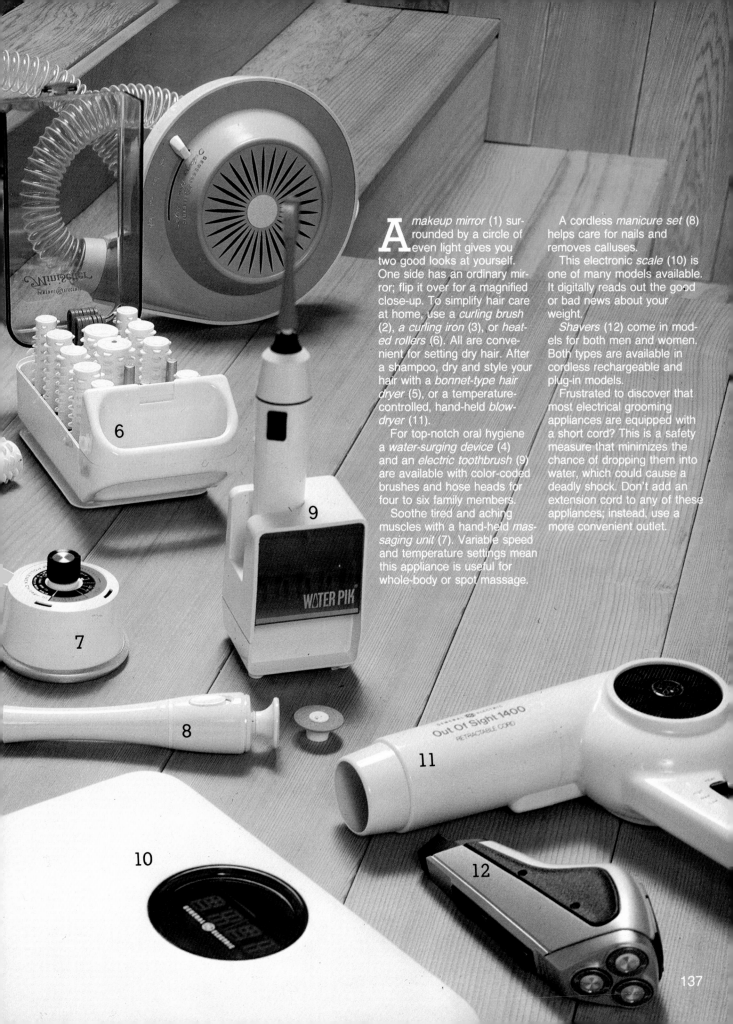

A makeup mirror (1) surrounded by a circle of even light gives you two good looks at yourself. One side has an ordinary mirror; flip it over for a magnified close-up. To simplify hair care at home, use a *curling brush* (2), *a curling iron* (3), or *heated rollers* (6). All are convenient for setting dry hair. After a shampoo, dry and style your hair with a *bonnet-type hair dryer* (5), or a temperature-controlled, hand-held *blow-dryer* (11).

For top-notch oral hygiene a *water-surging device* (4) and an *electric toothbrush* (9) are available with color-coded brushes and hose heads for four to six family members.

Soothe tired and aching muscles with a hand-held *massaging unit* (7). Variable speed and temperature settings mean this appliance is useful for whole-body or spot massage.

A cordless *manicure set* (8) helps care for nails and removes calluses.

This electronic *scale* (10) is one of many models available. It digitally reads out the good or bad news about your weight.

Shavers (12) come in models for both men and women. Both types are available in cordless rechargeable and plug-in models.

Frustrated to discover that most electrical grooming appliances are equipped with a short cord? This is a safety measure that minimizes the chance of dropping them into water, which could cause a deadly shock. Don't add an extension cord to any of these appliances; instead, use a more convenient outlet.

STORAGE PIECES

If the storage in your bath consists of little or nothing more than an overcrowded medicine cabinet, you already know how it can become annoyingly cluttered and even dangerous. Pages 128-131 show ways to build in the storage you need. Here we offer a selection of storage units you can buy.

How you incorporate needed storage into your bath depends on how presentable your bath items are and how accessible you want them to be.

A variety of bath organizers exist: a freestanding *magazine rack* (1), a *makeup organizer* (2), a self-stick *soap-and-shampoo rack* (3), and a freestanding *towel rack* for guest towels (4). Open storage units tailored to hold specialized appliances such as a blow dryer (8) also are available.

If there's no room for your personal effects in your existing medicine cabinet, consider adding a modern-lined unit (5).

A *cotton-ball dispenser* (6), (7), and *makeup case* (9) keep small items under cover.

Cleaning supplies and other bigger essentials need to be concealed, too. Choose one or several *circular stackable cabinets* (10), and you'll have convenient storage for cleansers, toilet paper, and children's bath toys. Toilet bowl brushes present special storage problems. A unit like the one shown here (11) keeps a brush handy, but out of sight; up top there's an ashtray and toilet paper dispenser. Every bath also needs a *wastebasket* (19) large enough to hold a day's accumulation.

Among the other special-
ized bathroom storage
devices on the market are:
swivel containers for tiny
items such as rings and contact lenses (12); *toothbrush
holders* (13); plastic and coat-
ed-wire *shelving* (14 and 15);
tissue dispensers (16); *shampoo racks* that hang from a
shower head (17); *undershelf
baskets* (18); and *interlocking
baskets* that allow you to
stack the units as high as you
like (20). Finally, if there isn't
any storage space left, you
might consider *swiveling trays*
(21). Because they roll around
on casters, you can keep
them in a nearby closet.

SHOWER AND BATH ACCESSORIES

Whether you take quick showers or indulge in luxurious soaks, bathing time can be a special pleasure with the accessories shown here. From an invigorating wake-up scrub with a loofah to an evening wind-down with a tub tray that holds your nightcap and bedtime story, the items *at left* make functional, practical, and attractive additions to your bath.

Any bath benefits from places to hang your robe, shower cap, and towels. *Hooks* (1) of all sizes and descriptions add hanging space wherever you need it and come in a wide range of colors. Attach hooks on a wall surface with screws or heavy-duty double-sided tape.

Brushes (2) are for scrubbing people, grooming hair, and cleaning fixtures. Choose your brushes carefully—good ones should last for years with proper care. Check to be sure bristles—either natural or synthetic—are well anchored and their relative stiffness is appropriate for the intended use. Natural bristle brushes distribute hair oil and remove dust better than synthetics, but man-made materials are easier to clean. Look for brushes with sturdy handles and comfortable grips. Clean your brushes after each use—rinse in cool water, air dry, and store by hanging on a hook.

Natural sponges (3) are expensive, but long-lasting and pleasant against the skin. Rougher-textured *loofahs* (4) help remove dead skin cells while bathing. Brushes and mitts made of natural materials stimulate blood circulation and give skin a healthy glow.

A *rubberized bath mat* (5) grips the tub bottom with suction cups to prevent slips.

A *bath tray* (6) fits most standard tubs and has compartments to hold a beverage, brushes and soaps, and a stack of reading material.

For the ultimate bath, a *portable whirlpool device* (7) turns a standard tub into a mini-spa. (More about whirlpools on pages 116 and 117.)

A *toilet brush/container* (8) solves the problem of storage after use. This smartly designed container holds the brush upright for drying.

141

Finally, stock your bath
with personal care prod-
ucts to cleanse and
pamper yourself, as well
as with hardworking
cleaners for your bath's
surfaces. Here's a selec-
tion of suggestions. And
for more about keeping
your bath at its best, see
the chapter that follows.

Soap commercials lead us to believe that the right soap will make us younger-looking, more popular, and more successful. One thing you can believe is that soap will definitely make you cleaner.

An emulsifying agent, soap works as a solvent that dissolves oil and dirt. The trick is to find one that does this without also dissolving too much of the skin's protective layer of natural oil. Here your choices are many—superfatted soaps with extra creamy lather, non-allergenic types for sensitive skins, medicated soaps, and delightfully perfumed formulations that pamper your senses in the bath. Whatever soap you choose will last longer if you keep it exposed to air so it can dry off between uses.

Soapy alternatives
Liquid hand and body soaps in pump-action dispensers replace messy soap bars, and are especially convenient in a bath used by several children. Both counter-top and hanging shower versions are available.

Bath salts and oils can make the water foamy, pleasantly slippery, or scented. You'll find a wide array of products with floral, fruit, vegetable, herbal, and mineral additives. Bubble baths just might coax a young, reluctant bather into the tub more often.

And consider how natural additives can enhance your bathing. For soothing baths, fill small muslin bags with your favorite herbs and hang them on the faucet. Essential oils of various flowers, leaves, and barks are also a bathing treat; a few drops add a pleasant fragrance to the bath water.

Cleaning aids
In addition, a well-stocked bath requires a team of cleaning products like the ones in the background here. Disinfectants come in both spray and concentrated liquid form. A spray-type tile and grout cleaner reduces the need for heavy scrubbing. An all-purpose foaming bath cleanser sanitizes and cleans enamel, porcelain, fiber-glass, and china fixtures.

In case you've wondered whether powdered or liquid cleansers work better in a bath, the answer is that both have their uses. Either is effective on tile and basins, and the abrasiveness of dry cleansers makes short work of stains on hard surfaces. The liquid type, on the other hand, makes better sense for surfaces that scratch more easily, such as paint and plastic laminate.

Window and mirror cleaners keep reflective surfaces shiny, and clear glass sparkling. Tank additives reduce mineral build-up and deodorize toilet bowls.

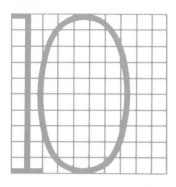

KEEP YOUR BATH AT ITS BEST

Have you ever been annoyed by a tub that just won't come clean, a faucet that drips no matter how hard you try to turn it off, or a toilet that gurgles incessantly? Problems like these bedevil every bath from time to time. Fortunately, none is difficult to cure. All you need are a few spare moments, a few simple tools and supplies, and the know-how presented on the following pages. This chapter also delves into two other important topics—how to customize a bathroom for a disabled person, and how to make sure your bath is as safe as it should be.

ROUTINE MAINTENANCE

What's the secret to keeping a bath sparkling clean? Getting the entire family involved by encouraging each member to give the bath a quick wipe-down after his or her morning routine. For convenient cleanup, assemble a kit of detergent, glass cleaner, disinfectant bathroom cleaner, brushes, and cloths or paper towels, and keep the kit in an easy-to-reach spot so everyone will be tempted to use it.

Even young children can get in the habit of wiping the sink, tub, and counters with a damp sponge after each use. Of course, you'll still need to periodically scrub with liquid detergent to remove tough soap residue, but a daily rubdown keeps surfaces looking fresh.

Air dry the shower curtain or door immediately after each use. If necessary, wipe it down with a towel to absorb excess moisture. If mildew does form on a shower curtain, launder it in the washing machine along with some old towels to serve as scrub brushes. Use mild detergent and set the temperature control on cool.

Walls, mirrors, and accessories usually need moisture and dust wiped away several times a week.

After you empty bathroom waste containers, wash with a disinfectant and dry well before returning them to the bath—or line them with plastic bags and simply toss out the bags.

Check the toilet bowl, tank, and exposed pipes daily to see if they're due for cleaning. A disinfectant bathroom cleaner helps you get through this admittedly unpopular chore as painlessly as possible.

Sweeping, mopping, and/or vacuuming bathroom floors regularly can stall off a major floor cleaning and polishing for many weeks.

TO CONTROL MOISTURE AND HUMIDITY

Baths, even those without showers, generate lots of humidity. Poor ventilation promotes mildew, peeling paint, rust, and lingering, musty odors. Excessive moisture can also reduce the effectiveness of insulation and may even damage ceilings, rafters, beams, and the roof.

The Home Ventilating Institute and the U.S. Department of Housing and Urban Development recommend that bathroom exhaust fans be capable of changing the air at least eight times per hour (more about this on page 93). When operating the unit, be sure to keep the bathroom door closed; otherwise, hot, moist air could penetrate the rest of the house.

Doesn't opening a window do the same job as turning on a fan? The answer is yes, of course, but usually not as well. And in cold weather, a window that's continually open, even if just a crack, wastes expensively heated house air. If your bath doesn't have a fan, consider that adding one could pay off in energy savings, as well as increased comfort and lower humidity levels.

CLEANING BATHROOM SURFACES

	REGULAR CARE	SPOT AND STAIN REMOVAL	SPECIAL TREATMENT
WALLS AND CABINETS			
Paint and wall coverings	Wash in small sections with detergent solution.	Use degreaser on oily spots and stains.	Use baking soda and water paste, or commercial cleaner.
Prefinished	Dust regularly; use wax or oil-type polish; wipe with grain.	Treat sticky, oily spots with appliance cleaner/wax.	Avoid using too much water on wood; always wipe dry.
Ceramic tile	Wipe clean with a mild detergent/water solution.	Use baking soda paste or grout cleaner; blot and rinse.	Avoid harsh cleaners and abrasive cleansers.
FLOORS			
Resilient	Dust-mop, sweep, or vacuum; damp-mop as needed.	Scrub with mild detergent or appliance cleaner/wax.	Use polish with sealer on porous types.
Carpeting	Vacuum daily.	Use aerosol cleaner or absorbent cleaning powder.	Check colorfastness; avoid excess water; dry quickly.
Hard-surface tile	Dust-mop; vacuum; damp-mop as needed.	Use cleanser or washing soda on greasy spots.	Finish unprotected tiles with oil-base sealer.
COUNTERS			
Plastic laminate	Wipe with damp sponge, using mild detergent solution.	Baking soda/water paste will draw out most stains.	Avoid abrasive cleaners; protect with appliance wax.
Wood	Damp-sponge; dry. Avoid too much water.	Use 50% ammonia solution; fine steel wool on scratches.	Keep wood from drying out; refinish unprotected areas.
Hard-surface tile	Wipe with detergent solution; dry.	Degreaser on oil-based spots; special cleaner on tile grout.	Creamy liquid wax provides an easy-to-clean tile finish.
FIXTURES AND FITTINGS			
Baked-on enamel	Wipe down with mild liquid detergent; rinse.	Mild abrasive and nylon brush on soap/mineral deposits.	Treat gently; abrasives will eventually remove the finish.
Fiber glass	Wipe down with soft cloth; dry. Don't use abrasive cleansers.	White automotive compound removes occasional stains.	Restore shine with liquid or paste auto wax.
Metal	Use mild liquid soap and water; wipe dry.	Abrasive cleanser will remove most stains.	For rust and tarnish try automotive chrome cleaner.
Vitreous china	Use mild liquid detergent; rinse and dry.	Cream of tartar paste removes mineral buildup/stains.	Strong abrasives can permanently etch the surface.

PLUMBING REPAIRS

Like doctors, plumbers don't like to make house calls anymore—they seem to prefer that you bring your ailing pipes to the office. Fortunately, you don't really need a plumber for the most common plumbing ills; they're less distressing than the common cold. To cure them you need only a few special tools, patience, and a little know-how. Pages 146-149 explain how to cope with the most common bathroom plumbing difficulties— clogged drains, malfunctioning toilets, and leaky faucets.

SOLVING DRAIN PROBLEMS

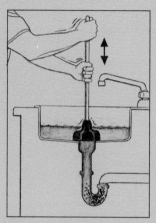

If the flow down a drain is merely sluggish, try running hot water for about 10 minutes to dissolve clogged soap or grease. If this fails, try a commercial drain cleaner. Caution: Don't use drain cleaner with a completely clogged drain. If it doesn't work, you'll have to dismantle the trap and deal with dangerously caustic water inside.

Unclogging sinks
Remove the stopper and clean out hair, soap bits, and other debris. Fit a plunger with a molded suction cup over the drain opening and seal tightly, as shown *upper left*. Plug the overflow outlet with a cloth, then work the plunger up and down to dislodge the obstruction.

If plunging doesn't work, crank a drain auger down the drain, as shown *lower left*. Thread it down through the trap, or open the cleanout at the bottom of the trap and work up from there. If this doesn't do the job, remove the trap, as explained below, and work your auger into the main drain.

Unclogging a tub
As with balky sink drains, chemical drain cleaner might free a *slow* tub drain, but don't attempt using chemicals with one that's completely stopped up. Instead, remove the *pop-up stopper* as shown *upper right* and try threading an auger down the drain. If this doesn't work, you may have to remove the *overflow* assembly and auger through the blockage as shown *lower right*.

Dismantling a trap
Clogged drains and missing rings or contact lenses make it likely that you'll have to take apart a trap at some time or other. When you must, first shut off the water or remove faucet knobs to prevent an accident while the drain is open. Put a bucket underneath to collect

water lodged in the trap. Now loosen slip nuts on either side of the trap; it will drop loose or come off with a tug. Some versions have only one slip nut; loosen this, then turn the trap to unscrew it from the drainpipe.

When reassembling, take care not to overtighten the fittings. Turn by hand, then go another quarter-turn with a wrench. To test the refitted trap for leaks, fill the basin with water, then open the drain and check all connections for moisture.

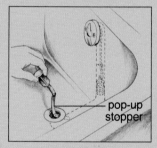

pop-up stopper

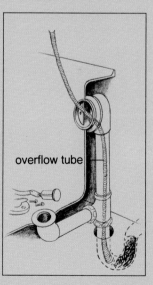

overflow tube

FIXING TOILETS

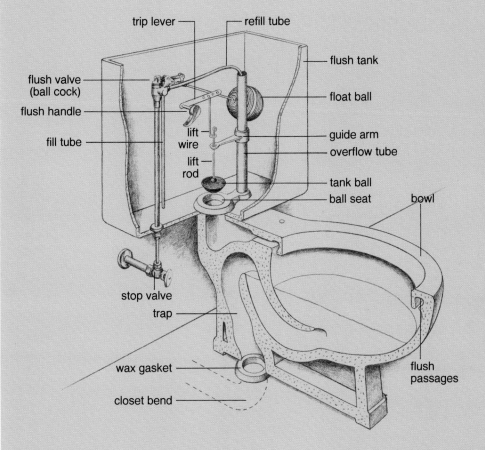

trip lever — refill tube

flush tank

flush valve (ball cock)

flush handle

float ball

fill tube

lift wire

guide arm

overflow tube

lift rod

tank ball

ball seat

bowl

stop valve

trap

wax gasket

flush passages

closet bend

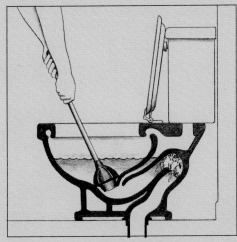

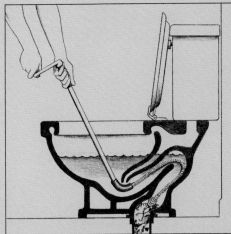

The anatomy drawing *upper left* shows the internal workings of a typical toilet. Flip the *flush handle*, and a chain reaction occurs. The *trip lever* lifts up the *tank ball*. As water rushes down through the *ball seat* and *flush passages* into the *bowl*, the *float ball* drops until the rod it's attached to opens the *flush valve*. This lets more water into the tank through a *fill tube* and refills the bowl through an *overflow tube*. When the float rises to the tank's full position, the valve closes, completing the cycle.

If you hear a steady trickle of water running from the tank through the bowl, first lift the float ball. If the flow stops, try bending the ball's rod downward slightly. A ball that's more than half submerged is leaking and must be replaced.

Next, observe the tank ball as the tank empties. Adjusting its linkage or replacing the ball will stop water leaking into the bowl.

Finally, check the flush valve. Shut off water to the toilet and dismantle the valve. Inside you'll find a seat washer similar to the one shown in the first column on page 148. A new washer will stop the leak.

To clear a stopped-up toilet, use a plunger over the hole in the bottom, as shown *at far lower left*.

If a plunger doesn't work, use a special snake called a *closet auger*, illustrated *at near lower left*. As you crank, it wends its way through the passages.

147

PLUMBING REPAIRS
(continued)

FIXING LEAKY STEM FAUCETS

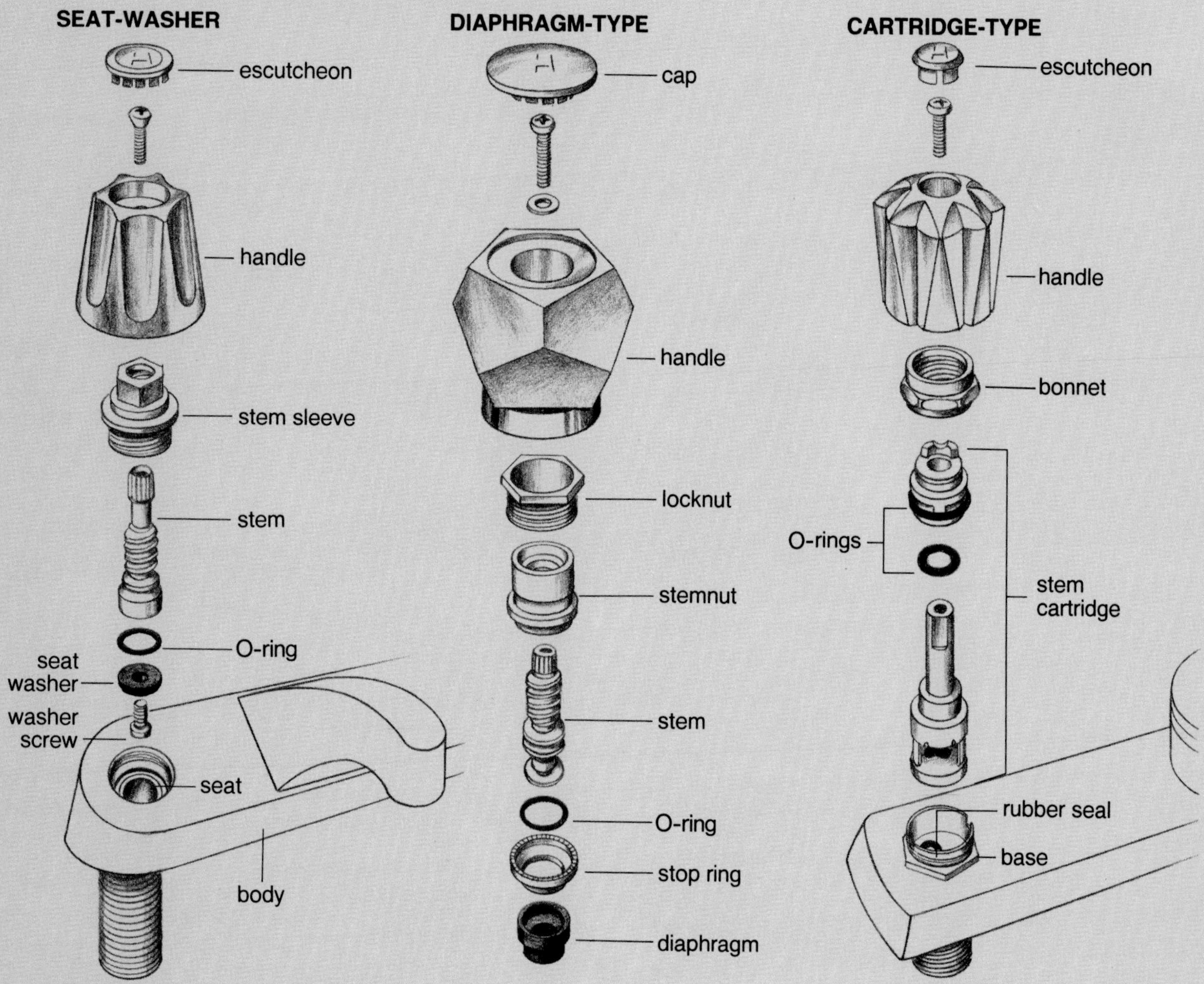

SEAT-WASHER

escutcheon

handle

stem sleeve

stem

O-ring

seat washer

washer screw

seat

body

DIAPHRAGM-TYPE

cap

handle

locknut

stemnut

stem

O-ring

stop ring

diaphragm

CARTRIDGE-TYPE

escutcheon

handle

bonnet

O-rings

stem cartridge

rubber seal

base

Stem faucets always have separate controls for hot and cold water and may be any of the three types shown in exploded views *above*. To dismantle these, first pry off the decorative *escutcheon* on the handle. Back out the screw and remove the handle by lifting it straight up. Remove the nut underneath with an adjustable wrench or a pair of slip joint pliers, then turn out the stem.

At the bottom of the stem you'll find a *seat washer*, *diaphragm*, or *cartridge*. Replacing these and any *O-rings* will usually stop dripping.

With older, washer-type faucets, the seat may have worn and may need regrinding. You can do this with a simple, hand-operated seat cutter available at most hardware stores. Older faucets also typically use string-like, rosin-impregnated packing in place of O-rings. This should be replaced every time a faucet is dismantled.

If your faucet has a swiveling spout, and the spout oozes water from its base, try slightly tightening the nut there. If that doesn't stop the leak, remove the spout and replace the O-ring inside.

If you have old-fashioned, washer-type faucets that need frequent attention, consider replacing them with the diaphragm or sleeve-cartridge types shown here, or the single-lever models shown *opposite* and discussed on page 87.

FIXING ROTATING-BALL AND DISK FAUCETS

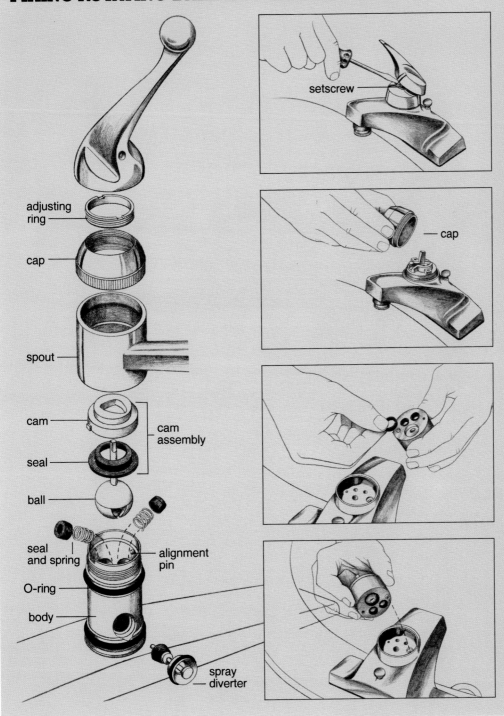

adjusting ring

cap

spout

cam

cam assembly

seal

ball

seal and spring

O-ring

body

spray diverter

alignment pin

setscrew

cap

Inside every rotating-ball faucet, a slotted *ball* sits atop a pair of spring-loaded rubber *seals* (see exploded view *at far left*). Raise the faucet handle and the ball rotates so its openings align with the supply line ports, allowing water through.

When a rotating-ball faucet begins to drip, its springs and seals are probably giving out. To get at them, shut off the water supply and dismantle the faucet. Insert a lead pencil into each seal; the seal and spring will grip the pencil so you can easily withdraw them. If the handle is leaking, either the *adjusting ring* has loosened or the *seal* above the ball is worn.

The workings of a disk faucet include a pair of ceramic disks. Raising the handle causes the upper disk to slide across the one below, letting water through. The disks themselves rarely need replacing, but their inlet ports can be restricted by minerals.

The drawings *at near left* show how to take apart a disk faucet. Shut off the water source. Pry off the cap, then remove the screw and handle. Remove the screws holding the cartridge in place and lift out. Check to be sure that the inlet ports are clear (they can be scraped with a pocket knife), that dirt hasn't lodged between the disks, and that the inlet seals are in good condition. If they're worn, replace them as shown.

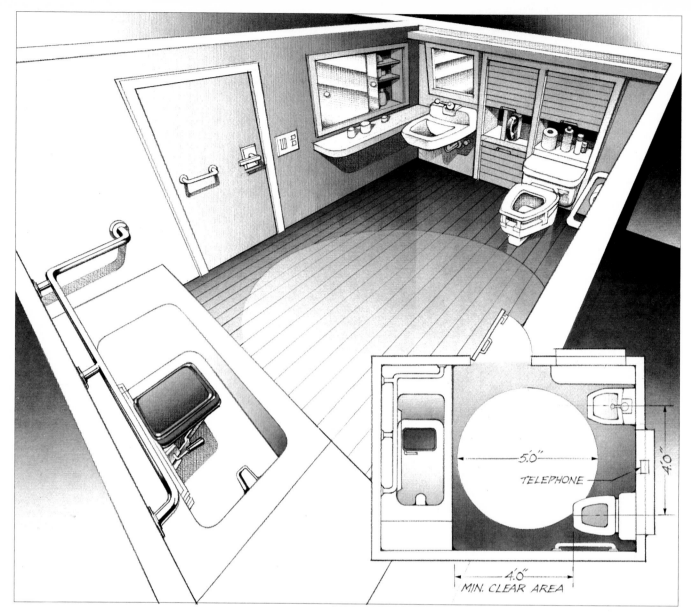

5.0"

TELEPHONE

4.0"

4.0"

MIN. CLEAR AREA

The first person to consult about modifying or remodeling a bathroom is the disabled person who will use it. He or she is best qualified to determine what's essential for comfort and convenience. This rundown probably constitutes the ideal facility for a disabled person; the number of changes you'll actually have to make will depend on the specific needs of your family.

Before you decide that your present bathroom will never work for a wheelchair-bound person, compare its measurements with these standards from the Veterans Administration and check the drawing *above*.

• Provide a clear area at least 5 feet in diameter inside the bathroom. This space enables a wheelchair-user to rotate the chair and move freely to each of the fixtures.

• Provide a clear area 4 feet wide in front of each fixture to accommodate the full length of the wheelchair. When toilet and sink are along the same wall, separate them by 4 feet of free wall space to simplify transferring from the chair to the toilet.

• Provide a toilet seat between 19 and 20 inches off the floor (standard seats are 15 to 16 inches).

• The lavatory should be no higher than 34 inches off the floor and should extend 27 inches from the wall.

• Plumb water supply pipes and drainpipes in a horizontally offset position, or relocate them inside the wall, to free knee space beneath the lavatory.

• Insulate the hot water supply pipe and drainpipe to prevent burning a wheelchair-user's knees.

• Provide a shower measuring at least 4 feet square that has a front opening at least 36

inches wide. The shower stall should have no threshold to impede the wheels of the chair.

• Provide grab bars for support when transferring from wheelchair to toilet or into and out of the tub or shower. Locate the bars so that their central handhold is 33 inches off the floor.

• The door to the bathroom must swing outward rather than inward and should be fitted with a lever-type handle, not an ordinary knob.

The VA also suggests including the following items in a bath for the disabled: thermostatic controls for the water supply to the tub or shower to prevent sudden changes in water temperature; a bathroom telephone for use in emergencies; and vanities no taller than 34 inches.

OUTFITTING
FOR A DISABLED
PERSON

Small-scale changes

After you've compared your existing bath with these suggested measurements, you may think that everything that could be wrong *is* wrong. Realize, though, that it's not always possible *or* necessary to meet each and every design standard. Depending on how well a particular disabled person can function in your existing bathroom (with some assistance, perhaps), you might be able to improve conditions with just a few alterations.

Here are some ways to avoid a complete redo.

• If the doorway cannot be widened to allow passage of the wheelchair, consider the user's parking the chair outside the bathroom and transferring to a smaller rolling chair for inside-the-bath mobility. Provide grab bars near the doorway to the bathroom.

• If the shower stall is not wide enough to accommodate a wheelchair, another chair or bench can be located inside the stall. Again, grab bars will be necessary.

• If the bathroom is equipped with a tub, use a bench that straddles the tub to enable the disabled person to sit in the tub at wheelchair height. A hand-held shower head and a shower curtain or folding shower door will allow the individual to shower while sitting.

• Outlets, switches, and storage that the wheelchair-user requires must be within his or her limited reach.

• Use a wedge-shaped shim to angle the mirror for viewing from a seated position.

• A seat attachment can raise the seat of a conventional toilet. Well-placed grab bars also

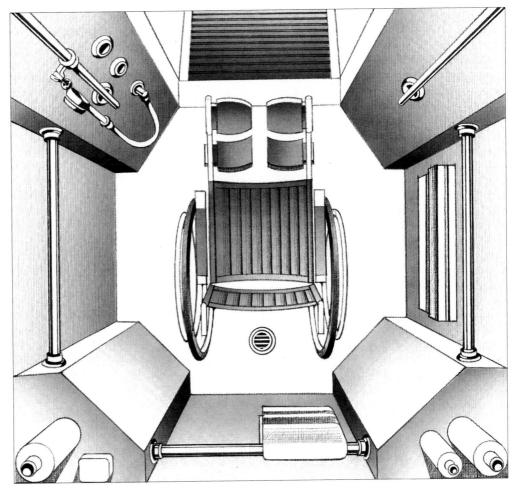

aid in transferring from a chair to a normal-height toilet seat.

• Paddle-type or single-lever fittings may replace hard-to-handle faucets.

Bigger changes

When permanent changes are scheduled, here are several ways to minimize the cost.

• Instead of installing a new toilet or built-up seat, consider removing and reinstalling your present floor-mounted toilet on a wooden, fiber-glass, or ceramic shim that will raise it several inches off the floor.

• Lower an existing wall-hung lavatory and give it additional

support with heavy-duty brackets.

• Remove or modify vanities. Removing the center doors may allow a wheelchair-user to pull the wheelchair or a small rolling chair right up to and under the sink.

A complete bath remodeling

Should you decide to completely remodel your existing bath, you'll have a variety of

fittings and fixtures to choose from. Special sinks—longer and shallower than most—are designed especially for use by people in wheelchairs. Some ready-made shower units are large enough to accommodate a roll-in chair, as shown *above*. Medical supply companies are a good source for many of the products you'll want to consider—everything from grab bars to hydraulic lifts that use water pressure to lower and raise a seat into and out of the bathtub.

HOW SAFE IS YOUR BATH?

Accidents in the bath account for about 25 percent of all household mishaps. Slips, falls, and hot water burns head the list. By definition, accidents are unexpected events, but a little foresight and planning can prevent many of them. Use these safety checklists to see how safe your baths are. Correct any deficiencies you find, and make your bath a safer place for the whole family.

An inventory of the ideal bathroom would include these safety features:
• Grab bars located within each bathtub and shower stall.
• Soap dishes in tub and shower permanently installed and recessed, so there's no chance of bumping your head or a limb during a fall.
• Faucet parts that are shatter-resistant and have no sharp edges.
• Faucet sets in shower/tub combinations mounted 30 to 34 inches above the bottom of the tub so you can reach them from either a seated or a standing position.
• Faucet sets for showers mounted 48 to 52 inches above the bottom of the tub—the ideal height for a person standing.
• A shower head mounted 69 to 72 inches from the bottom of the tub or shower. Even a shower head could serve as a grab handle if you slip.
• Hinges for tub/shower swinging enclosure doors placed on the end that is opposite control valves.
• A shower stall light in a vapor-proof fixture, with the switch at least 6 feet away from the shower stall.
• Shower and tub enclosures of impact-resistant safety glass or acrylic plastic.
• Non-breakable tumblers in the bathroom. In fact, try to avoid any glass in bathrooms.
• A bathroom door that, when it opens, clears fixtures and individuals using any fixtures.
• Towel bars or rings located 6 inches or less from the entrance to a tub or shower.
• Water temperature that is no higher than 115° F.
• Passage hardware on the bathroom door that is unlockable from both sides of the door so you can get in to rescue a child or injured person.

• A lavatory counter that has room for toothbrush, razor, soap, and other appliances and accessories.
• Slip-resistant flooring material.
• Slip-resistant strips on the floor in front of the lavatory and tub, where water is likely to spill.
• Switches for lights, ventilating fans, heaters, and other fixtures located well away from water sources.
• Provision for a night-light.
• An auxiliary heat source permanently installed and controlled by a switch.
• Sun and heat lamp fixtures controlled by a timer switch.
• An electrical outlet installed at the mirror but well away from water outlets. Today's codes require that any outlet installed in a bathroom be protected by a ground fault circuit interrupter, a device that instantaneously shuts off power to a faulty circuit. In a bathroom, the wrong combination of water and electricity could be fatal.
• Provision for razor blade disposal.
• Any breakable containers kept in cabinets or on wide shelves or counters.
• Scatter rugs securely anchored with pads or double-face tape.
• Area lighting at the mirror for makeup, shaving, and other personal care.
• A first-aid kit kept in an easy-to-reach spot.

CHILDPROOF YOUR BATH

Playing in and around water is a favorite activity among children. Combined with the privateness of the bath, child's play could lead to mishaps if certain precautions are neglected.
• Put safety latches or locks on cabinets that hold potentially dangerous materials—cleaning supplies, drugs, mouthwashes, and cough syrups. Putting dangerous substances on a high, unsecured shelf is an inadequate precaution; kids can climb to reach forbidden fruit.
• Paint the lids of all potentially dangerous substances bright red so children can learn to avoid these substances by the color. Stickers from poison control centers and civic organizations also warn children.
• Insist that all drugs come with childproof lids or other packaging that is difficult to open.
• Provide a sturdy step stool to raise your child high enough to easily reach faucets and counter tops.
• Be sure towel bars are within a child's reach—a rod at the right height may even prompt a kid to hang up the towel.
• Light controls should be where a child can easily reach them. Use a night-light.
• Be certain that the hot water temperature is regulated. Little ones scald easily.

Better Homes and Gardens® Books

Would you like to learn more about decorating, remodeling, or maintaining your baths? These Better Homes and Gardens® books can help.

Better Homes and Gardens®
NEW DECORATING BOOK
How to translate ideas into workable solutions for every room in your home. Choosing a style, furniture arrangements, windows, walls and ceilings, floors, lighting, and accessories. 433 color photos, 76 how-to illustrations, 432 pages.

Better Homes and Gardens®
COMPLETE GUIDE TO HOME REPAIR,
MAINTENANCE, & IMPROVEMENT
Inside your home, outside your home, your home's systems, basics you should know. Anatomy and step-by-step drawings illustrate components, tools, techniques, and finishes.
515 how-to techniques, 75 charts, 2,734 illustrations, 552 pages.

Better Homes and Gardens®
STEP-BY-STEP
BASIC PLUMBING
Getting to know your system, solving plumbing problems, making plumbing improvements, plumbing basics and procedures.
42 projects, 200 illustrations, 96 pages.

Better Homes and Gardens®
STEP-BY-STEP
BASIC WIRING
Getting to know your system, solving electrical problems, making electrical improvements, electrical basics and procedures. 22 projects, 286 illustrations, 96 pages.

Better Homes and Gardens®
STEP-BY-STEP
BASIC CARPENTRY
Setting up shop, choosing tools and building materials, mastering construction techniques, building boxes, hanging shelves, framing walls, installing drywall and paneling. 10 projects, 191 illustrations, 96 pages.

Better Homes and Gardens®
STEP-BY-STEP
MASONRY & CONCRETE
Choosing tools and materials, planning masonry projects, working with concrete, working with brick, block, and stone, special-effect projects. 10 projects, 200 drawings, 96 pages.

Better Homes and Gardens®
STEP-BY-STEP
HOUSEHOLD REPAIRS
Basic tools for repair jobs, repairing walls and ceilings, floors and stairs, windows and doors, and electrical and plumbing items.
200 illustrations, 96 pages.

Better Homes and Gardens®
STEP-BY-STEP
CABINETS AND SHELVES
Materials and hardware, planning guidelines, the ABCs of cabinet construction, cutting and joining techniques, project potpourri.
155 illustrations, 96 pages.

Other Sources of Information

Manufacturers and professional associations provide valuable assistance to the consumer by offering educational materials, catalogs, and other information for the asking. Most professional associations publish lists of their members, and will be happy to furnish these lists upon request.

American Home Lighting Institute
230 N. Michigan Avenue
Chicago, IL 60601
Membership includes manufacturers, distributors, and retailers of residential lighting fixtures. The institute also trains lighting specialists.

American Standard
Box 2003
New Brunswick, NJ 08903

Eljer Plumbingware
No. 3 Gateway Center
Pittsburgh, PA 15222

Kohler Company
Highland Drive
Kohler, Wisconsin 53044

National Association of the Remodeling Industry (NARI)
11 E. 44th Street
New York, NY 10017
Membership includes contractors, manufacturers, wholesalers, lenders, utilities, and publishers. The association promotes the common business interests of the remodeling industry.

National Kitchen and Bath Association (NKBA)
114 Main Street
Hackettstown, NJ 07840
Members have agreed to abide by and practice the bylaws and codes of ethics for the kitchen/bathroom industry.

National Spa and Pool Institute
2000 K Street NW
Washington, DC 20006

Tile Council of America
Box 326
Princeton, NJ 08540
Membership includes manufacturers of ceramic tile. Booklets are available on how to best use ceramic tile, as well as information on do-it-yourself installation.

ACKNOWLEDGMENTS

Interior Designers and Architects

The following is a page-by-page listing of the interior designers, architects, and project designers whose works appear in this book.

Cover
  Stephen Mead Associates
Pages 6-7
  Moon Brothers Design and Construction
Pages 8-9
  Perez Associates, Inc.;
  William Dutcher, A.I.A.
Pages 10-11
  Dean Graves, A.I.A.
Pages 12-13
  Robert and Sandra Woodward;
  Emily Ann Smith
Pages 14-15
  Metzler, Muirheid and Wright
Pages 20-21
  Bil Wischmeyer;
  Jon Bruton
Pages 22-23
  Sento Hot Tubs, Inc.
Pages 24-25
  Daniel Feidt
Pages 26-27
  Gerry Maccartee;
  William Becze
Pages 28-29
  Ted Peterson;
  William Becze
Pages 30-31
  Milton, Schwartz,
  Jim Burns
Pages 32-33
  Ernst Dorfi;
  Howard Kaplan
Pages 34-35
  Nickel-Fay Associates
Pages 36-37
  Jane Juliet; Paul Juliet
Pages 38-39
  Jon L. and Kerry T. Austin
Pages 40-41
  Elayne Mordes;
  Thomas H. Olson, Design Unity; Merle H. Sykors, Design Unity

Pages 42-43
  Win Mass-Protzen
Pages 44-45
  Stephen Glassman, Art & Architectural Design;
  Minky Morfit
Pages 46-47
  Bruce Levy;
  Paden Prichard
Pages 48-49
  Thomas L. Thomson;
  Case Construction Co., Inc.;
  Stephen Mead Associates
Pages 52-53
  Jerry Ross;
  Janis Lee
Pages 56-57
  Robert V. Duncan;
  David Ashe, The Design Concern
Pages 60-61
  David W. Durant;
  Robert V. Duncan;
  John Reagan; Sandra Boles
Pages 104-105
  Wayman Design
Pages 106-107
  Sandra Miller
Pages 108-109
  Weeks-Davis and Associates, Inc.;
  H. James Weber, A.I.A.
Pages 110-111
  Environmental Design Class, University of Minnesota School of Architecture
Pages 114-115
  Ilan Amatai;
  John Barksdale, Law, Woodson, Barksdale
Pages 118-119
  Dennis Blair
Pages 120-121
  Kevin Walz
Pages 122-123
  William Kohanek

Pages 124-125
  Peter M. Fine
Pages 126-127
  Stephanie and Roberta Interiors;
  McGuire/Engler/Davis Architects
Pages 128-129
  Daryl Hansen;
  William Lecky/Cooper-Lecky Partnership
Pages 130-131
  Marilyn Worseldine;
  Ted Peterson;
  David Ashe, The Design Concern
Pages 132-133
  Developmental Resources;
  The Houseworks;
  Lloyd Jafvert;
  Marsha Longstaff

Photographers and Illustrators

We extend our thanks to the following photographers and illustrators, whose creative talents and technical skills contributed much to this book.

Peter Bosch
Ernest Braun
Ross Chapple
Mike Dieter
Jim Downing
Peter M. Fine
Harry Hartman
Hedrich-Blessing
Hellman Design Associates, Inc.
Bill Helms
William N. Hopkins
Bill Hopkins, Jr.
Fred Lyon
Maris/Semel
E. Alan McGee
Frank Lotz Miller
Chris Neubauer
Bradley Olman
Jessie Walker
Sandra Williams

Associations and Companies

Our appreciation goes to the following associations and companies for providing information and materials for this book.

Allibert
American Standard
Armstrong Cork Company
Barney's Chelsea Passage
Beylerian
Braun
Caswell Massey
The Chicago Faucet Company
Clairol
Closet Maid Corporation
Cutler Corporation
Delta
Eljer Plumbingware
Flexco Textile Rubber Company
Formica Corporation
General Electric
H.U.D.D.L.E.
I.D.G.
Ingrid Ltd.
InterDesign Craft Inc.
Jacuzzi Whirlpool Bath
Kartell U.S.A.
Kohler Company
Martex/WestPoint Pepperell
A.Y. McDonald
Moen, Stanadyne, Inc.
NuTone Division of Scovill
Plumb Supply
Renovator's Supply
Rubbermaid Inc.
J.P. Stevens
Teledyne Water Pik
Tile Council of America, Inc.
Universal Rundle Corporation

FIXTURE TEMPLATES TO HELP YOU PLAN

½ BATHS

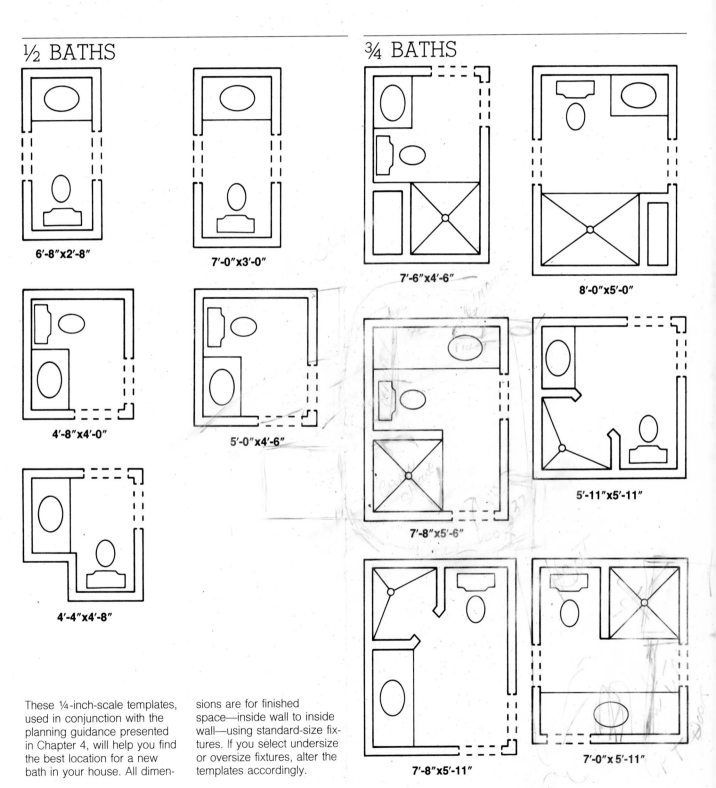

6'-8"x2'-8"

7'-0"x3'-0"

4'-8"x4'-0"

5'-0"x4'-6"

4'-4"x4'-8"

¾ BATHS

7'-6"x4'-6"

8'-0"x5'-0"

7'-8"x5'-6"

5'-11"x5'-11"

7'-8"x5'-11"

7'-0" x 5'-11"

These ¼-inch-scale templates, used in conjunction with the planning guidance presented in Chapter 4, will help you find the best location for a new bath in your house. All dimensions are for finished space—inside wall to inside wall—using standard-size fixtures. If you select undersize or oversize fixtures, alter the templates accordingly.

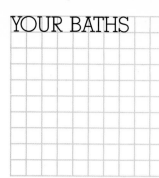
FIXTURE TEMPLATES TO HELP YOU PLAN
(continued)

FULL BATHS

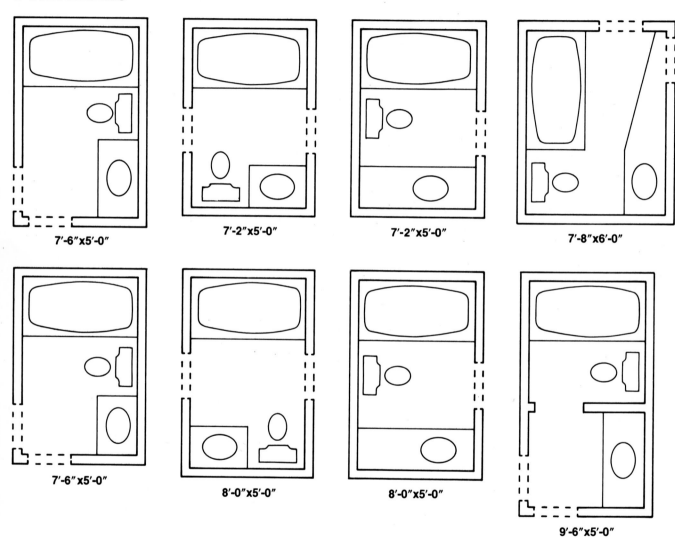

7'-6"x5'-0"

7'-2"x5'-0"

7'-2"x5'-0"

7'-8"x6'-0"

7'-6"x5'-0"

8'-0"x5'-0"

8'-0"x5'-0"

9'-6"x5'-0"

FULL BATHS

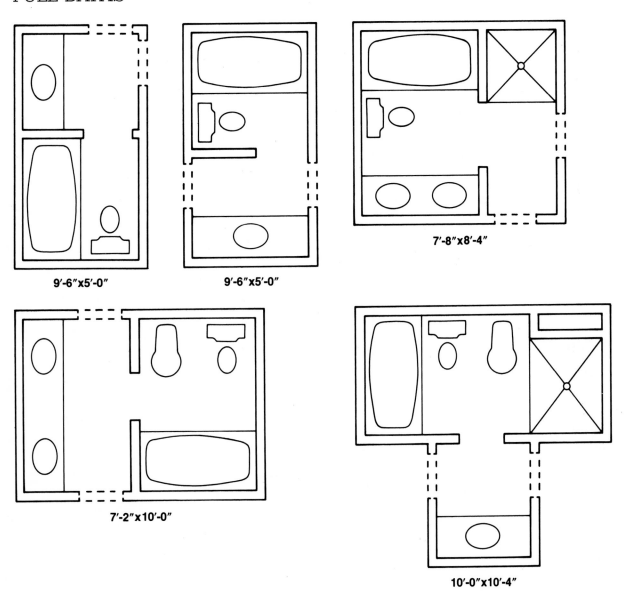

9'-6"x5'-0"

9'-6"x5'-0"

7'-8"x8'-4"

7'-2"x10'-0"

10'-0"x10'-4"